TALES FROM ALABAMA PREP FOOTBALL

Ron Ingram
Rubin E. Grant

SportsPublishingLLC.com

ISBN-10: 1-59670-059-9
ISBN-13: 978-1-59670-059-8

Publishers: Peter L. Bannon and Joseph J. Bannon Sr.
Senior managing editor: Susan M. Moyer
Acquisitions editor: John Humenik
Developmental editor: Travis W. Moran
Art director: K. Jeffrey Higgerson
Dust jacket design: Kenneth J. O'Brien
Interior layout: Kathryn R. Holleman
Photo editor: Erin Linden-Levy

Printed in the United States of America

Sports Publishing L.L.C.
804 North Neil Street
Champaign, IL 61820
Phone: 1-877-424-2665
Fax: 217-363-2073
SportsPublishingLLC.com

Library of Congress Cataloging-in-Publication Data

Ingram, Ron.
Tales from Alabama prep football / Ron Ingram, Rubin E. Grant.
    p. cm.
  ISBN 1-59670-059-9 (hardcover : alk. paper)
  1. Football--Alabama--History. 2. School sports--Alabama--History. I. Grant, Rubin E., 1957- II. Title.
  GV959.52.A43I54 2006
  796.332'6209761--dc22
                        2006020100

I dedicate this book to the boys and men who bring so much honor and pride to their communities each Friday night in the fall. And I dedicate it to the families, like my own, who support those who keep the spirit alive each year.

—*Ron Ingram*

To my late parents, Albert Tyler and Delorious Grant, for letting me become a sports fanatic as a boy, and taking me to Carver-Montgomery High School football games to foster a passion for the sport.

To my wife, Dena, and our daughter, Krystal Joy, for understanding that working nights and sometimes weekends is a way of life for a prep-sports writer and for occasionally proofreading some of my stories.

To my church family, especially Judy Anderson and Sallie Dewberry, for their prayers, support, and encouragement.

To the sports staff at the Birmingham Post-Herald *who enabled me to develop as a writer, made my stories read better, and were dedicated to putting out a quality product each day.*

And to all the Alabama high school football players, coaches, administrators, fans, and readers who made what I was doing worthwhile.

—*Rubin E. Grant*

CONTENTS

ACKNOWLEDGMENTS

Covering high school football in the state of Alabama has been a privilege for the past 30 years. I grew up playing high school football in this state, and I have witnessed the impact it has made on the lives of the many young men who bear the heat of August to wear their school uniforms with pride.

As a sports writer, I have seen some courageous efforts through the years and some strange events. I have seen winners and losers walk off the field better men because of this great game.

It has been a labor of love for me. I still get excited at the smell of freshly cut grass on a hot September Friday night. The bands blaring in the background still give me chills. And when the whistle blows and the game begins, I feel like a kid again at least for a few hours under the lights. I can't thank my own coaches enough for their influence on my life.

My family—God blessed me with a wonderful wife and mother for my two beautiful daughters—has been understanding and supportive of my chosen profession. Although they might not always understand my passion, they have encouraged me in my endeavor to chronicle this part of American history and lore.

The Birmingham News, Dothan Eagle, Dothan Progress, and the *Brundidge Banner* have allowed me to continue to be a part of this drama for more than three decades. Each has played a part in keeping my passion alive. I thank each. Many thanks go to the archives of the *Birmingham Post-Herald, Montgomery Advertiser, Mobile Register, Huntsville Times,* and the Alabama State Department of Archives that still houses numerous other small, now defunct publications that detailed this phenomenon called high school football. Special thanks also go to the Alabama High School Athletic Association, Alabama

Sports Hall of Fame, and state high school sports historian Bill Plott for his help in this project.

High school football is a great game. It's also a great stage for young boys to become young men. The coaches who mold these youngsters are some of the finest this state and nation have to offer.

—Ron Ingram

INTRODUCTION

The year was 1996. High school football in Alabama reached new heights when teams began traveling the "Road to the Birmingham" for the Super 6 Championships at historic Legion Field, the "Football Capital of the South." But long before then the sport already was considered a religion in the state.

On Friday nights in communities throughout the "Heart of Dixie," entire towns showed up to watch their boys play—in such places as Carbon Hill, where Lloyd Nix, who quarterbacked Auburn to its only national championship in 1957, honed his skills; and Sulligent, where Joe Cribbs became a two-time *Parade* prep All-American.

"The atmosphere was absolutely the best," Nix said of his high school playing days. "We had about 2,200 folks living in Carbon Hill, and 2,100 were at the ballgames. They followed us everywhere we went."

"Football was always big in Sulligent," Cribbs said. "It's pretty much that way in any small town in Alabama. Everybody in town would be at the game, and it was an opportunity to display your talents in front of everybody."

In *Tales from Alabama Prep Football*, you will visit some of those places and learn about some of the legends of the sport, such as Bo Jackson, Bobby Bowden, and Vince Dooley, who got their starts on high school playing fields in the state. You will discover what kind of player Terrell Owens, the infamous "T.O.," was in high school and why a few folks believe 2005 NFL Offensive Rookie of the Year Carnell "Cadillac" Williams was a better high school running back than Bo.

You will read about Green Bay Packers' Super Bowl hero Bart Starr as a high school quarterback at Sidney Lanier in Montgomery; how Kenny "Snake" Stabler got his moniker; and how Heisman Trophy winner Pat Sullivan was a standout in three sports at John Carroll Catholic in Birmingham before he wound up as a record-setting quarterback at Auburn University.

You will become acquainted with some of the state's legendary prep coaches who were better known by their nicknames: "Snitz," "Hot," "Big Train," "Pea Soup," and "Snake Eye." You will find out how the state's winningest coach, Glenn Daniel, got into the profession by accident.

As you weave your way through *Tales from Alabama Prep Football*, you will encounter some of the great Alabama football families, such as the Goodes, Singtons, Neighbors, and Castilles. You will come across some of the state's dynasties, including the Tuscaloosa Black Bears' streak of 64 consecutive games without a loss in the Roaring '20s, Tallassee's record-setting streak in the 1950s, and Clay County's record 55-game winning streak in the 1990s.

Tales from Alabama Prep Football will also tell you about the great rivalries, such as the "Clay Bowl" (Clay County vs. Lineville), which was judged one of the nation's 10 best high school rivalries by *USA Today* and *Sports Illustrated*, "The Battle for Murder Creek" and black school rivalries before integration.

This volume details memorable games and performances, such as the night more than 42,000 fans came to Legion Field (and several thousand more were turned away) in 1974 to watch the clash between Banks High School, featuring its star quarterback Jeff Rutledge, and Woodlawn, with its stellar running back Tony Nathan. You will discover how University of Alabama coach Paul "Bear" Bryant caught Cornelius Bennett's high school coach, Steve Savarese, in the buff while recruiting the Ensley High standout, and how legendary home run hitters Hank Aaron and Willie Mays traded football for baseball.

Tales from Alabama Prep Football will give you a revealing and enjoyable glimpse into the rich high school football heritage in the state.

—Rubin E. Grant

LEGENDS

BO KNOWS STARDOM

The year Vincent Edward "Bo" Jackson came out of McAdory High School in McCalla, he wasn't regarded as the top running back in the state. Enterprise running back Alan Evans was rated ahead of Jackson among the Class of 1982 college prospects—with good reason.

Jackson was a do-everything player for McAdory and carried the ball approximately 10 times a game. He never gained more than 1,000 yards in a season. He came close his senior year, rushing for more than 900 yards and scoring 17 touchdowns.

"We didn't have many athletes," said Dick Atchison, Jackson's high school coach. "Bo had to play all over the place. We couldn't just utilize him on offense. He never came off the field. He played offense and defense. He was our kick returner and punt returner, our place-kicker and punter. He won several games for us kicking field goals. He wore flat-nosed kicking shoes, so he came out to change shoes.

"The play I remember the most happened when we were playing Leeds in the Dental Clinic [Classic] at Legion Field. We were playing

Bo Jackson takes a handoff from quarterback Scott Davis during practice.
Courtesy of Dick Atchison

Bo at fullback. We tossed the ball to tailback Edwin Mack on a sweep, and Bo was out front blocking. He put four guys down on the ground, and Edwin ran 75 yards for a touchdown. Bo told me that was one of his favorite plays, too.

"Another time we were playing Pleasant Grove, and Bo was playing defense. They ran the option and Bo tackled the quarterback, but he made the pitch. Bo was on the ground but got up and tackled the running back for a 2-yard loss.

"We saw things like that happen over and over. He was an amazing athlete. He could do so many things well. If we had put him in the 'I' as the tailback and let him go, there's no telling what his stats would have been."

If it had been left to Bo's mother, Mrs. Florence Bond, he would not have played football at all.

"I sure didn't want him to play football," the late Mrs. Bond said, following Jackson's junior year at McAdory. "It's just so rough. I didn't want him to get hurt."

Jackson, who earned the nickname "Bo" because he was as stubborn as a wild boar, didn't listen to his mother. That's not too surprising. He once said he was the "John Gotti" of his neighborhood. Bo didn't listen to his three older brothers, either. They tried to convince him to play just baseball, the sport he began playing when he was 10.

"They said I wouldn't succeed in three sports, that I should stick with one and stop trying to impress my friends and people in the community," Bo said as a high school junior. "I told them I was going to do it, that it was none of their business what I did."

Bo also excelled in baseball—he set a then-national record with 20 home runs during his senior year—and track—he was a two-time state decathlon winner—but signed a college football scholarship with Auburn University. Evans also signed with Auburn, but it was Jackson who became the Tigers' featured back, and in 1985 he won the Heisman Trophy.

He eventually became a two-sport star in the National Football League and Major League Baseball and was a sports icon as a pitchman with his "Bo knows" commercials for Nike.

"PAPA BOWDEN"

In the shadows of a goalpost at Woodlawn High School in Birmingham in the 1940s was a house with a garage in the backyard. Some bushes behind the fence of the football field separated the garage from the stadium, preventing the folks who lived in the house from watching a game for free.

But that didn't stop a young Bobby Bowden and his dad from taking in the action. "We would get on top of the garage and watch it," Bowden said. "That's where I first learned about the game."

Since that elementary introduction to football, Bowden has gone on to become the winningest coach in college football and winner of two national championships at Florida State University.

Before his lengthy coaching career, Bowden was a star running back at Woodlawn High in the late 1940s. He has fond memories of his high school playing days. "It was one of the greatest experiences I've ever had," Bowden said. "When you get to my age, you start looking back over your life, and I think that sort of set me on this road."

Bowden didn't play football his first two years at Woodlawn because of an illness. "I had been sick with rheumatic fever in 1943," Bowden recalled. "Back in those days, they didn't know much about it, so my parents wouldn't let me play football." Instead Bowden joined the high school band and played trombone. He had learned to play the trumpet earlier in his boyhood.

Finally, during his junior year, Bowden became a member of the Colonels' football team. He played the role of quarterback in their offense. "Hardly nobody ran the T-formation," he said. "Everybody ran the single wing or the Notre Dame box. I played tailback, right halfback, and left halfback. We had leather helmets and did not have face guards. There were a lot of one-tooth athletes. I was lucky not to be one of them, but I had my nose broke."

High school football was big in Birmingham (as well as the rest of the state). "We had the Big-5 city high schools," Bowden remembered. "There was Woodlawn, Ramsay, Phillips, Ensley, and West End. We played about eight games. We'd play the other Big-5 schools, we always played Bessemer, and we would go to Montgomery to play Sidney Lanier. At the end of the year, the top two teams from the Big 5 would play. That was the big game. It was played on Thanksgiving and it started off with Birmingham-Southern [College] and Howard College, but after the war [World War II], the Birmingham-Southern and Howard game was dropped. We'd get around 27,000 for the game. One year we got 38,000. It was a big event. If you won it, you could start to strut a little bit."

Bowden went from Woodlawn to Howard College (now Samford University) and became a Little All-American. He began his college coaching career at Howard, then went to West Virginia and took over at Florida State in 1976, and turned the Seminoles into a national power.

From Alabama *HS. 50ish* *Georgia 64-88*

DANDY DOOLEY

In the *New Georgia Encyclopedia*, Vince Dooley was described "as a short-tempered, irascible youngster" while growing up in Mobile. Thanks to the football coach at McGill Catholic High School (now McGill-Toolen), the petulant Dooley found something to keep him from a life of working in the Mobile shipyards. He turned to athletics.

"My football coach, Ray Dicharry, helped point me in the right direction," Dooley said. "I have a great deal of respect for him, steering me to sports. Sports made sense to me."

Dooley was a two-sport star at McGill, playing football and basketball. "Most people said I was a better basketball player than football player. What they were saying was I wasn't worth a darn playing football," Dooley said laughingly. "I was a pretty good basketball player. I held a couple of state records. I enjoyed basketball more than football."

On the gridiron, Dooley was a hotshot quarterback. He was named the starting quarterback as a sophomore and led McGill to the Mobile City championship in 1949.

"We ran the T-formation and I was the quarterback, then we would shift to the single wing, and I was the spinner back at fullback," Dooley recalled. "The fullback took a lot of snaps. I did the same thing at Auburn. To stretch a point, I was All-State in football. I'm sure I was All-State in basketball."

Dooley continued to play both sports in college. "I started as a sophomore in basketball and football, then I tore my knee up," he said. "I hurt it during the football season and reaggravated it during basketball and had to have surgery. If we had the scope back then, I would have been back, but they took out the cartilage, and I couldn't play any more."

Dooley entered the Marines after college, and it was almost by happenstance that he became a coach. "After I got out of the Marines, I had to decide what I wanted to do," he said. "I was thinking about going into the banking business or staying in the Marines or coaching.

There was a great opportunity for me to go coach at Auburn, so that's what I did.

"I learned the importance of a coach when I was in high school, how to relate to a player and the importance of helping kids because they are at a formative age."

Dooley never coached in high school. In 1964 at age 31, he was hired as head football coach at Georgia and remained the Bulldogs' head coach until 1988. He won 201 games, six Southeastern Conference championships, and a national championship in 1980, securing his place in the College Football Hall of Fame.

HANNAH DEFINES OFFENSIVE LINEMAN

Once described by Paul "Bear" Bryant as the "best lineman I ever coached," John Hannah lived up to that high praise and then some as a pro blocker for the New England Patriots.

A selection into the College and Pro Football Halls of Fame, Hannah admits he was born to play football. His dad Herb played at the University of Alabama, and his younger brothers Charlie and David each followed dad and older brother to Tuscaloosa.

Upon retirement, John spent his time watching college and pro football—still keeping his keen attention on the blockers in the trenches.

His start in football was anything but meager. He weighed 11 pounds at birth in 1951. He weighed 35 pounds when he was a year old and 210 pounds by the time he was in the eighth grade.

His dad Herb not only played for the Crimson Tide, but also spent time in the NFL with the New York Giants.

Hannah was a high school phenom at Baylor Prep in nearby Chattanooga, Tennessee, for three seasons. Big John returned to Alabama to play his final year of prep football at Albertville, where his family owned a farm.

He earned All-State and Super All-State as an Aggie, but he didn't stop there. He also set a state record in the shot put in track and was the state heavyweight wrestling champion.

Vince Dooley, while at McGill in Mobile. *Courtesy of McGill-Toolen High School*

Bryant also described Hannah as an intense but well-mannered Southern gentleman who remembered "his raising." Hannah's college career was also a smashing success—literally. Nicknamed "Ham Hocks," he was an SEC champion in the shot and discus and was unbeaten his freshman year as a wrestler.

Football, however, was Hannah's game.

A three-time All-SEC guard and two-time All-American, he won the Jacobs Trophy as the SEC's best blocker in 1972 as well as the Lombardi Trophy as the nation's best lineman. He played in the Hula Bowl as a senior and then was considered the best college lineman in the College All-Star Game—a 14-3 loss to the NFL-champion Miami Dolphins.

He reported to the Dolphins as the No. 1 pick in 1973 at 6 feet, 2 inches, 265 pounds—small by today's standards. But 13 seasons later, he was called the greatest guard to ever play in the NFL and was chosen as one of the NFL's 100 greatest players at the end of the 20th Century. Hannah was chosen the NFLPA Offensive Lineman of the Year three consecutive years from 1978-81. He played in Super Bowl XX in 1985 versus the Chicago Bears in his final season.

John discounted any lack of size. "When you are shorter, you probably have a little leverage advantage," he told Boston reporters who doubted his abilities in 1973.

Known for his intense work ethic and durability, he also shared his philosophy of the game, which he credited to his college coach Bryant.

"Bear Bryant taught us how to win when I was at Alabama," he said. "He inspired you to give your maximum effort on every play. He told us that usually a game is decided by only four or five plays. You never know when those plays are coming, so you have to be ready on every play."

When he first signed his pro contract in 1973, he donated his entire signing bonus to former Tide teammate John Croyle's Big Oak Ranch, a home for homeless children. The money was used to build a house at the ranch, which is still aptly named "The Hannah House."

He became the first Patriot to be selected to the Pro Hall of Fame (1994), the first year he was eligible. He was inducted into the Alabama Sports Hall of Fame in 1988. Hannah also was named to the University of Alabama's "All-Century Team" and was named to John Madden's NFL "Millennium Team."

Buck Buchanan

PARKER'S BIG MAN BECOMES NFL GIANT

Junious "Buck" Buchanan, born in 1940, grew up in Birmingham in the 1950s. The star football and basketball player at A.H. Parker High School didn't attract recruiting interest from the University of Alabama or Auburn University. Those schools were not recruiting black athletes at the time.

Down the road in Louisiana, however, Grambling College's Eddie Robinson was eager to get the gangly, 6-foot-7 Buchanan in his school. He'd heard enough of Buck from his high school coach, Major Brown. Brown was a trusted source of recruiting information for any interested black college coach at that time.

Parker, once listed as the largest predominantly black high school in the nation, didn't just play local teams. The Thundering Herd traveled throughout the Southeast to other big cities, such as Atlanta, Nashville, and New Orleans. The basketball team did much the same.

But scholarships were still few and far between, so Robinson offered Buck an "If" scholarship. Robinson saw something special in Buck Buchanan—just as Major Brown had promised. But still, all he could offer was "If you are good enough to play, I will give you a scholarship."

Buchanan started out playing both basketball and football. Eventually he settled on football—going both ways on offense and defense at end. By the time his career was over, Robinson called him "the finest tackle I have ever seen."

He was an integral part of the college all-star team in 1963 that shocked the NFL-champion Green Bay Packers in a preseason exhibition contest.

In 1963, Buchanan became the first player chosen in the American Football League (AFL) draft. He was selected by the Dallas Texans, who later moved and became the Kansas City Chiefs.

As a strong, 280-pound man who not only had size and strength but speed to boot, Buchanan helped revolutionize the game, becoming the prototype NFL defensive lineman.

He was the original "Iron Man," missing only one regular-season game in his 13-year career—all with the Chiefs, playing in 166 straight games at one stretch. Buck helped Kansas City reach two Super Bowls—including Super Bowl I—and played with the Chiefs' Super Bowl IV champions in 1969.

His sack of Green Bay quarterback Bart Starr, another Alabama native, from Montgomery, was the first in Super Bowl history.

Once his playing days were over, Buck spent three years as an assistant coach in the NFL, two at New Orleans and one at Cleveland. He returned to his beloved Kansas City where he became a successful businessman and civic leader. He died after battling cancer in 1992.

Buchanan was considered one of the game's most dominant defensive linemen for eight straight seasons—earning either AFL All-Star or NFL Pro Bowl honors from 1965-72. He was pegged the Chiefs' MVP in 1965 and 1967. He played in the Pro Bowl three times.

In 1987, he was inducted into Alabama's storied Sports Hall of Fame.

In 1990, Buck was inducted into the Professional Football Hall of Fame—becoming the first AFL defensive lineman to be enshrined.

He started two businesses in Kansas City, All-Pro Construction Co. and All-Pro Advertising. His numerous civic activities included his role as a founder of the Black Chamber of Commerce, where he served as president from 1986-1989. He also headed the state's Special Olympics effort.

"I remember the things the NFL players were saying about the AFL, and it hurt. They said things like calling us 'Mickey Mouse'," Buchanan said at his Hall of Fame induction. "I was proud to be in that first Super Bowl. But the real pride came when we won Super Bowl IV. It was so different. We went into that game knowing we would win."

In 1999, the Buck Buchanan Award was established in the former NAIA All-American's honor. It is presented annually to the NCAA's Top Division I-AA defensive player.

Ozzie Newsome
71-73 H.S.

THE WIZARDRY OF OZZIE

In an era in which the forward pass was sometimes an afterthought, Ozzie Newsome was a record-setting receiver at Colbert County High School in Leighton. Newsome set the state record for receptions in a season with 80 and touchdown catches in a season with 23 while playing for the Indians from 1971-73.

"We ran the wishbone, but we threw out of it," Newsome said. "We utilized the downfield passing game. Phil Gargis was the quarterback, and Pat Flanagan was the other end. We were scoring over 30 points a game. I always could catch the football. That's one reason why Coach [C.T.] Manley started me as a sophomore."

Newsome helped Colbert County win a state championship during his junior season in 1972. "He was a great high school player," said Gargis, who was a senior that season. "He developed every year. When he came in, he was undersized and skinny. He was quiet and pretty intense, but he was always full of jokes."

Playing for the Indians was always one of Newsome's goals because of Colbert County's rich tradition. "We were basically a football powerhouse," Newsome said. "I grew up hoping to play on the varsity. After my freshman year and going through spring training, Coach Manley allowed me to work with the first team, and he let me do the same thing during summer camp. That sort of propelled my career."

Newsome's career took him to the University of Alabama, where he became an All-Southeastern Conference receiver while playing in the wishbone under legendary coach Paul "Bear" Bryant.

"I could have gone from Leighton to any number of schools that would have thrown me any number of balls," Newsome said. "But for me, the No. 1 thing was winning. I think in three years of high school ball and four years of college, I was on teams that wound up losing only eight or nine games in all that time. I embraced the opportunity to win rather than individual stats."

Newsome's stats were phenomenal in his 13 seasons in the NFL with the Cleveland Browns. He set a NFL record for tight ends with 662 career receptions, securing a spot in the Pro Football Hall of Fame. Currently, he's the general manager of the Baltimore Ravens.

SMALL-TOWN FARM BOY MAKES IT BIG TIME

Lee Roy Jordan grew up on a farm in south Alabama, and just because he played football didn't mean one of his siblings was going to do his chores for him. "My dad didn't let football interfere with my chores," Jordan said. "As the fourth boy, I got to do all the bad details, the grunt work, such as feeding the hogs and cows."

Jordan transferred the hard work on the farm to the football field, largely because of his Excel High coach, W.C. Majors. "Coach Majors laid the groundwork for my work ethic," Jordan said. "He believed the harder you worked, the better you played. I was like that at Alabama and I was like that with the [Dallas] Cowboys. I believed you were supposed to go full speed every step on every play."

Jordan didn't get a chance go half-speed at Excel because the school didn't have many players. "We were not a very big school," he said. "Everybody who came out for the football team got to play. We had only 18 or 19 guys who could dress out. We were a small [Class] 1A school. Our big rival was Monroe County High School from Monroeville, and Frisco City. We'd also play big-city schools, such W.S. Neal from Brewton and Satsuma and Bay Minette."

With so few players, Jordan had to play a variety of positions. "I was playing linebacker and fullback and tailback and quarterback and anything else we needed," he said. "You played the whole game. If you got hurt, you couldn't come out because there was nobody else to go in.

"I weighed 190 pounds, so I was a good-sized lad. I was the only one of the boys in my family who weighed over 150. I was 6 foot, 190 pounds. All of my growing took place after my sophomore year. I gained 30 pounds and grew two or three inches."

Jordan might have been overlooked by the major colleges if it were not for an opposing player. "We were playing against the team over in Brewton and coach Jerry Claiborne, who was an assistant under Coach [Paul] Bryant at Alabama, came to watch a fullback for them," Jordan recalled. "I was a junior and I had a pretty good game. Coach Claiborne came over after the game and told me they'd be back the next year to see me, and they did."

Jordan went to Alabama and was the defensive leader of the Crimson Tide's 1961 national championship team. In 1962, he was an All-America linebacker. The Cowboys selected him in the first round of the 1963 NFL draft and he became the team's starting middle linebacker his rookie season. He anchored the Cowboys' rugged "Doomsday Defense" for 15 seasons, was a perennial All-Pro selection and played in two Super Bowls, collecting a championship ring in Dallas' 1972 victory against the Miami Dolphins.

LATE-BLOOMING STALLWORTH

John Stallworth's ascension to the Pro Football Hall of Fame almost didn't get off the ground. Integration, however, gave him a boost.

According to Stallworth, as a freshman at all-black Druid High School in Tuscaloosa, he was told he was too small to play. So Stallworth transferred to predominately white Tuscaloosa High shortly after schools in the state began desegregating in the late 1960s.

"I still wanted to play football, so I just started going to Tuscaloosa High," Stallworth said. "I had an elder brother who also played at Tuscaloosa High. We felt size-wise we could play there."

Stallworth was 5 foot 11 and weighed between 150 and 160 pounds. "I was a tall, skinny frail kid," he recalled. He joined the Tuscaloosa team as a junior. Although he thought he was best suited to play receiver, he wound up playing defensive end, a position, he said, "I didn't understand anything about playing it."

Tuscaloosa changed coaches before Stallworth's senior season and he figured that was his chance to finally play receiver. Instead, the new coach, Harold "Red" Lutz, told him he wanted to keep him at defensive end. "He said, 'We don't have anybody to throw you the football,'" Stallworth remembered. "He said they could put me in the backfield and hand me the football, so I changed to running back my senior year."

Stallworth doesn't recall how many yards he gained that season, but he said he was not a 1,000-yard rusher on a struggling team. "As far as winning football games, we didn't do too well," he said. "I played two years and we won two games."

Despite Tuscaloosa's losing ways, Stallworth developed as a player. "That was my first venture into organized football," he said. "I came back from the experience realizing I could play and realizing I had a love for the game."

Stallworth was selected to play in the Alabama high school All-Star football game the summer following his senior year, and that gave him an indication about what kind of player he was. "I was fortunate to compete in the high school All-Star game," he said. "I was able to compare myself with some other good players. It gave me confidence."

By graduation, Stallworth had grown to 6-2, 174 pounds. He signed a football scholarship with Alabama A&M University thanks to his high school teammate, Sylvester Croom, now the head football coach at Mississippi State University. "I was very fortunate in that regard," Stallworth said. "I was the tailback and Sylvester was the fullback. Sylvester's father, Rev. Croom, was instrumental in me going to A&M. He was an A&M grad and I asked him to talk to the coach at A&M and he did."

Stallworth went on to become Alabama A&M's all-time leading receiver with 103 career receptions and was a two-time All-Southern Intercollegiate Athletic Conference selection. The Pittsburgh Steelers chose Stallworth in the fourth round of the NFL draft. He played 14 seasons with the Steelers, teaming with Lynn Swann for several seasons to give Pittsburgh the best receiving combo in the league at the time. Stallworth set Steelers records for receptions (537), receiving yards (8,723) and touchdowns (63), and collected four Super Bowl championship rings to secure his place in the Pro Football Hall of Fame.

THE ITALIAN STALLION

To hear Johnny Musso tell it, he was just an average high school football player who happened to play for a great coach in a great program in Birmingham.

"I had a great time at Banks," Musso said. It was a really good program and was at its peak when I was there [in the mid-1960s]. It was a great experience. I was not very big. I was 165 pounds as a sophomore and 180 as a senior. It was always fun to play at Legion Field. I played for a really good high school coach. He taught us to be fundamentally sound."

George "Shorty" White said, "That's just Johnny being Johnny." He described Musso as "some kind of player."

"If you met Johnny in person, even back then in high school, you would not know he played football," White said. "He was a humble, soft-spoken person who you loved to be around. But on the football field, he was a totally different person. He was hard-nosed and tough. He was like a cobra, he'd strike you before you knew you had been struck. He was quick and strong for his size.

"I remember when he was a freshman, he weighed 135 pounds. He was playing strong safety—I couldn't imagine him playing strong safety at that size. I was working with him on his reads and techniques and I could tell he was a quick learner. Before he started gaining weight—he was about 145 at the end of his freshman year—I had a talk with his mother and I told her I wanted her to do something to get him bigger. I told her to feed him five meals a day. I also told her I was teaching summer school, and when it ended at 12 o'clock, I was going to be down in the weight room and I wanted Johnny to meet me there. I was younger then and could still lift that metal, and Johnny was trying to catch me with bench presses and squats. I had two leg machines and he wore both of them out. Toward the end of the summer that rascal was up to 165 pounds, and that was big enough to play as a sophomore.

"He was good enough as a sophomore to be a part-time starter. I knew he would be the best running back I ever had. He wasn't the type of running back who would take it and go 75-80 yards, but if you wanted 10-15-20 yards, give it to him."

Musso's fondest memory of his high school career occurred when he was a sophomore and Banks was playing Woodlawn. "Both teams were undefeated and we were playing for the city championship," Musso said. "We won that game and went on to win the state championship. I was just an average guy. I was out there, but the seniors and juniors carried that team."

According to White, Musso downplayed his contribution. Banks would have lost if it wasn't for Musso's spectacular touchdown run. "He made the darnest run I've ever seen," White said. "We called a play off tackle and it was clogged up because Woodlawn had a big defensive end. Johnny started in there and we wouldn't have gotten a first down, but he bounced it outside. He reached the 5-yard line and they had a linebacker and defensive back with the angle on him, but Johnny just left his feet. They hit him, but he got in the end zone. That later became his trademark in college.

"There are not many Johnny Mussos that come your way."

In college at the University of Alabama, Musso was given the nickname "The Italian Stallion" because of his tough running style. He earned All-America honors in 1970 and 1971 and was Southeastern Conference Player of the Year in 1971. He rushed for 2,741 yards and 34 touchdowns in his career with the Crimson Tide and was inducted into the College Football Hall of Fame in 2000. He also played football in Canada and in the NFL with the Chicago Bears.

TONY NATHAN:
A ONCE-IN-A-LIFETIME PLAYER

Tony Nathan once scored seven touchdowns in a game, but that is not what he remembers most about his stellar career at Woodlawn High School in Birmingham in the early 1970s. In fact, his most memorable moment didn't even occur during a game.

"What I remember the most is before my senior year we were having a late-spring football camp at the school," Nathan said. "On the first day of practice, I got a concussion and missed the whole week. I was physically there, but not mentally. All I remember is my mother dropping me off and my mother picking me up."

Nathan, a running back, sustained the concussion after being tackled. "I was running with the football and somebody grabbed me from behind, spun me around and threw me down, and my head hit the ground. I got up and went back into the huddle, but when the rest of the guys went up to the line of scrimmage, I stayed in the huddle with my hands on my knees. That's when the coach figured I had a problem."

Nathan didn't have too many problems as an athlete at Woodlawn. He was a three-sport standout for the Colonels.

"I had a great time playing high school sports, baseball, basketball, and football," he recalled. "I tried track, but I wasn't fast enough," he added with a laugh.

"I wasn't trying to set any records or anything. I just played. I had a God-given ability, and I was doing something I enjoyed."

It was on the football field that Nathan made himself a star. His seven-touchdown game came in a 61-12 victory against Ramsay during his senior season in 1974. Also that season, Woodlawn played nearby Banks at Legion Field before more than 42,000 fans, the largest crowd to ever see a high school football game in Alabama. Nathan and Banks star quarterback Jeff Rutledge were the main attractions.

Nathan rushed for 112 yards in the game, but it took 31 carries. He also scored on a 13-yard run, but it came midway through the fourth quarter as the Colonels fell 18-7 to the Jets. "They played a better football game than us," Nathan said.

Dyer Carlisle, Banks' defensive coordinator at the time, designed his defense to contain Nathan.

"No one had stopped Nathan," Carlisle said. "We tried to keep him from getting on the corner, because if he did he was gone. There are only two times I've been on the field and I couldn't catch my breath. That's when Nathan had the ball and when Bo [Jackson] had the ball when I was an assistant at Southern Miss. Every time they got the ball my heart stopped."

George "Shorty" White, who was Banks' coach at the time, wishes he had a chance to coach Nathan in high school. "Nathan's record speaks for itself," White said. "If I had had him, we would have beaten everybody 70-0."

Jerry Stearns, who was an assistant at Woodlawn when Nathan was there and later became head coach, called Nathan a "once-in-a-lifetime" player. "He was a special athlete with all the things he could do," Stearns said. "He's the only high school player I've ever seen to hit a home run over the old scoreboard at Rickwood Field. On the football field, he was a lot bigger than people thought. He was 190-195 pounds. He wasn't a little scat back. People would break down to tackle him and he'd run over them. He was fast and strong. He had a quick first step, and he could stop on a dime and leave a nickel change."

"We would be in a game and people would be ooohing and aaahing about something Tony did. We saw him do so many incredible things in practice that when he did something in a game, he was just being Tony to us."

Nathan went on to the University of Alabama, where he was a two-time All-SEC back and was captain of the Crimson Tide's 1978 national championship team. He played nine seasons in the NFL with the Miami Dolphins and appeared in two Super Bowls. He's been an assistant coach at the pro and college levels since his playing career ended.

"BISCUIT" RISES TO GLORY

Early in his life, Cornelius Bennett was called "Fat Daddy." Then in the fourth grade, he was in the school lunchroom one morning eating breakfast and kidding around when somebody started calling him "Biscuit." The moniker stuck.

By the time he reached Ensley High School in Birmingham, "Biscuit" was being labeled a blue-chip football player. The only question was where to play him. He was tried at tight end, linebacker, and running back.

Steve Savarese, who came to Ensley at the outset of Bennett's junior season, wasn't sure what to do with him. "I was new and I didn't know where to play him," Savarese said. "It was trial and error. I played him at tight end because that's all he had played."

Eventually Savarese moved Bennett to running back because of the way Bennett ran the ball on the end around. "We saw what he did when he carried the football, and we came to a consensus to try him at running back."

Bennett blossomed in the backfield during his senior season, averaging 10.1 yards per carry while rushing for 1,099 yards and scoring 16 touchdowns. He also played linebacker and was among the team's leading tackles. "The thing I remember the most is his intensity," Savarese said. "He played every down with tremendous intensity, and it didn't matter where he played. He was a great team player. Besides his athletic ability, he was just a real lovable kid, a caring person. He was kind of like a mama's boy, but he loved to play the game.

"I'll never forget the first time Ensley beat Parker. They had used their last timeout and the clock was running out. Cornelius picked me up off the ground and kept saying, 'We're going to beat Parker, we're going to beat Parker.'"

Bennett also had a healthy appetite for soul food. He tried to get Savarese to try one particular delicacy. "Cornelius never had a driver's license," Savarese recalled. "I had to take him everywhere. Me, him and his brother went on a recruiting trip to Auburn, and Cornelius kept saying, 'Coach, let's stop and get some pig ears.' I told him, 'Cornelius, I'll take you to Burger King or McDonald's, but I ain't trying no pig ears.' Finally, we stopped at this soul food place. He got a couple of slices of bread and showed me how to eat ears, but I didn't try them."

Colleges recruited Bennett as a tight end, running back, and linebacker. "I'd prefer to play tight end," Bennett said at the time, "but if I have to play running back or linebacker, that's what I'll play."

Bennett signed with the University of Alabama and was put at linebacker, where he became a three-time All-American and won the Lombardi Award as the nation's outstanding college lineman. He spent 14 seasons in the NFL and was a five-time Pro Bowl linebacker with the

Buffalo Bills, Atlanta Falcons, and Indianapolis Colts. He played in five Super Bowls, four with the Bills.

MULTITALENTED AND MISUNDERSTOOD "T.O."

Flamboyant—Check.
Controversial—Check.
Athletically gifted—Check.
Great high school football player. Well, not exactly.

Terrell Owens, better known as "T.O.," often creates a firestorm with his antics on and off the field, but when he attended Benjamin Russell High School in Alexander City, he was better known as a basketball player and track star than a football standout. In fact, Owens didn't start for the football team until midway through his senior year.

"I remember when Terrell first started playing," said Steve Savarese, Owens' high school coach. "He would pull on my shirt and say, 'Coach, let me play.' I'd tell him, 'Terrell, you're not ready yet. You're not good enough.' He was so gangly, and as a football player he was just average."

But one thing Owens had going for him was desire, and that's something Savarese couldn't ignore. "He's a competitor," Savarese said. "He wasn't playing as much as he wanted to, but he wanted to compete."

Owens thought about quitting, but Savarese talked him out of it. "He was going to do some wrong things to make money," Savarese said, "but I took him to my house and let him work on cars."

After Owens' junior year, he and his mother went to Savarese demanding that he play more.

"They came to my office around lunch one day and I told him if he dedicated himself in the weight room and improved his work habits, he would get that chance. From that day on, he learned to work hard. He had a great senior year, but he didn't start until halfway through the year."

Few colleges noticed the lanky and speedy Owens. The University of Tennessee-Chattanooga went to Alexander City to recruit Benjamin

Russell's other receiver, Derek Hall, and Savarese convinced them to sign Owens. "I told them the Terrell I knew would come to the ballpark and give you all he's got," Savarese said.

Owens flourished with the Moccasins, despite playing for three head coaches. The San Francisco 49ers selected him in the third round of the 1996 NFL draft, and he became an All-Pro receiver on the West Coast before reaching the 2005 Super Bowl with the Philadelphia Eagles.

Savarese believes T.O. is misunderstood because of what he terms "other stuff," such as contract disputes, verbal battles with coaches and teammates, trash-talking with opponents and his infamous after-touchdown celebrations.

"I think he's a true competitor," Savarese said. "I think he showed that in the Super Bowl against the [New England] Patriots. In the game of professional football, you have to be part showman. When Terrell is on the field, it's strictly business. All that other stuff, he's just trying to have fun. He loves playing the game."

BORN TO RUN

If there was ever a player born to be a running back, it would be Linnie Patrick. At Walker County High School in Jasper, he had the classic running back body type, carrying 175 pounds on a 5-foot-10 frame. He had breakaway speed, running the 40-yard dash in 4.4 seconds. And he could run inside as well as get on the corners.

David Campbell, Patrick's high school coach, recalled the first time he saw Patrick run with the football. Patrick was in the ninth grade, playing for the junior high team.

"In his first game, he ran for four touchdowns in the first half, then he broke his pelvic bone [in the second half], and didn't play any more his ninth grade year," Campbell said. "In the 10th grade, we never had a lot of 10th graders play, but he looked good in fall practice and was a starter when the season began."

Patrick gained 1,965 yards as a sophomore and helped the Vikings reach the 1977 Class 4A championship game. As a junior, he averaged 11.9 yards per carry while rushing for 1,770 yards. As a senior in the fall of 1979, in a game against Berry High from Birmingham, he gained 372 yards on 32 carries, including touchdown runs of 8, 11 and 80 yards. He also had runs of 56 and 51 yards in the contest.

Following that performance, late Berry coach Bob Finley called Patrick "the best pure running back I ever saw. …" "He runs with power, speed, quickness, and moves," Finley said. "We did everything we could do defensively and couldn't stop him."

A confident youngster, Patrick said that was because of his running style, which he described as "running to daylight."

"The coach tells you how to run a play, but you have to read the defense," Patrick said. "I try to read the defense every game. If a hole I'm supposed to run to is not there, I run to daylight."

Patrick finished his career with a then-state-record 5,420 yards rushing. He was rated the No. 2 high school back in the nation behind Herschel Walker, who went on to win the Heisman Trophy while playing for the University of Georgia.

Patrick signed with the University of Alabama but was in and out of legendary Coach Paul "Bear" Bryant's doghouse. The highlight of his college career came when Bryant earned his 315th coaching victory to pass Amos Alonzo Stagg for most wins at the time. The Crimson Tide trailed archrival Auburn 17-14 entering the fourth quarter when Patrick ripped off a spectacular 31-yard run down to the Auburn goal line to set up Alabama's go-ahead touchdown. Later in the quarter, he scored a touchdown to clinch the Tide's 28-17 victory and hand Bryant the record.

CRIBBS STEPS INTO THE SPOTLIGHT

For the first few years of his professional career, Joe Cribbs was one of the top running backs in the NFL while playing for the Buffalo Bills. In his first season in 1980, he rushed for 1,185 yards and 11 touchdowns and was named the UPI AFC Rookie of the Year and was the only rookie starter in the Pro Bowl.

The following season he ran for 1,097 yards and three touchdowns and caught 40 passes for 603 yards and seven TDs.

He played two more years with the Bills, then jumped to the USFL, where he led the now-defunct league in rushing for two seasons while playing for the Birmingham Stallions. He returned to the Bills in 1985 and played five more years in the NFL, including two years with the San Francisco 49ers and a split season with the Indianapolis Colts and Miami Dolphins.

Cribbs traces his success in the pros to his high school days at Sulligent High, a small school in northwest Alabama near the Mississippi state line, where he was a two-time *Parade* All-American.

"When I was in high school, for me it was just a stepping point," Cribbs said. "I was extremely confident I could play at the next level. In high school, I could almost score when I wanted to. There were a lot of games I would score five or six touchdowns and the coach would tell me not to score any more. "I think I was a pretty unique player, but I can't say I was a legend." If not a legend, he was certainly a hometown hero. "Football was always big in Sulligent," Cribbs said. "It's pretty much that way in any small town in Alabama. Everybody in town would be at the game, and it was an opportunity to display your talents in front of everybody.

"I remember we played Russellville. We had 26 or 27 players, and they came out with 60 or 70 or more players. We were warming up and they circled the field. I remember Coach Ralph Ferguson telling me, 'They can play only 11 at a time.' I scored on a punt return and we won 21-20."

Tony Davis, the guidance counselor at Sulligent when Cribbs was in school, remembers Cribbs as a modest and quiet youngster. "He wasn't loud or boisterous," Davis said. "He was very polite, very sharp. He showed a lot of leadership through his quietness. Back in the early days of integration, he took a fair amount of verbal abuse, but he overcame it with class."

Davis also took note of Cribbs on the football field. "I have watched every game at the school for 37 years," Davis said. "Joe was the best athlete to ever come through Sulligent. He was a little ahead of his time. He had a gift. He would make a run in the middle of the field and they thought they had him hemmed in, then Joe would make a cut to the outside. Someone would have an angle on him in pursuit, but Joe was uncanny. He displayed a quick burst of speed when they thought he was running wide open. He always had something left.

"We were able to beat a lot of larger schools, like Russellville, because of Joe and his cousin James McKinney, who played quarterback.

"If Joe had been at a larger school, he would have gotten a lot more recognition. Sulligent is a small, out-of-the-way place. We didn't get a lot of newspaper coverage from anybody. But we remember Joe's contributions. We retired his jersey number 20 [in 2000]."

Cribbs took his talents to Auburn University, where he became the Tigers' all-time leading rusher with 3,368 yards, a mark since eclipsed by Bo Jackson, Carnell Williams, and James Brooks.

THE "DEUCE"

Almost a decade before he wowed University of Alabama football fans with his unimaginable moves and earned the nickname "The Deuce" because of his jersey number, David Palmer dazzled youth league fans as a boy.

Playing in the metro football Shug/Bear Bowl in Birmingham at Legion Field, dubbed the "Football Capitol of the South," Palmer caught a record six touchdown passes, showing off his amazing elusiveness.

By the time he arrived at Jackson-Olin High, he was already a legend, which grew during his career. Despite being only 5-8 and 170 pounds, Palmer played every skilled position on the field, including quarterback. He astonished fans and foes alike, leaving them in disbelief by what they had just witnessed.

"He's unbelievable," Jim Holifield, the then-coach of West End High in Birmingham, said during Palmer's senior season. "I really have no one to compare him to, except on the pro level with a guy I used to play against, Terry Metcalf. Palmer has those same types of moves that Metcalf had. Palmer's quick. He knows the average high school guy can't do anything with him."

Earl Cheatham, Palmer's high school coach, had difficulty explaining what Palmer did on the field. "I've run out of words trying to describe him," Cheatham said. "The boy has a lot of talent. He sees the whole field. He knows when to cut and when not to cut. Some people have him hemmed in and he just jumps out of the hole and into the clear. He's a little package of dynamite who may explode at any time. He amazes me at some of the things he does on the field."

Palmer also displayed a certain flamboyance, sporting a few gold chains around his neck, ala his idol Deion Sanders, who wore No. 2 in college at Florida State. "I'm not a showboat," Palmer said as a senior. "I have a lot of confidence. I believe any time I touch the ball I'm going to get a first down or score a touchdown."

Palmer gained 3,373 all-purpose yards and accounted for 42 touchdowns his senior season, leading Jackson-Olin to a 9-2 record, and was named the state's Mr. Football. At Alabama, he set the school record for receiving yards (217) in a game and played on the Crimson Tide's 1992 national championship team. He spent seven years in the NFL with the Minnesota Vikings.

THE SUPER RECRUIT

Richmond Flowers

Richmond Flowers Jr., was the original "Super Recruit."

The fabled track and football star became a superstar at the University of Tennessee and later an NFL return specialist for the Dallas Cowboys and New York Giants.

However, no one before him and few since have garnered the kind of attention this schoolboy drew when coming out of high school at Sidney Lanier in Montgomery.

There was good reason.

Flowers, who was elected to the Alabama Sports Hall of Fame in 2002, was a true prep phenom for the Poets. As a halfback, he was an All-Stater who attracted the attention of college coaches from California to Maine. As a track star, he was unparalleled in Alabama prep history. Ironically, he is best remembered for the courage he displayed in the one race he lost.

The focus of a national recruiting battle boiled down to LSU, Alabama, and finally Tennessee. Flowers didn't make up his mind until just before August practice was to begin. His recruiting focus was chronicled almost daily in the state's biggest newspapers, such as *The Birmingham News* and *Montgomery Advertiser*. He landed at Tennessee where he went on to become an NCAA track champion and SEC football star.

He certainly lived up to his billing in college. He was an NCAA hurdles champion and was chosen All-SEC by his sophomore year in football. He would go on to play for the Cowboys.

It was in high school where the legend began, however, making Flowers a folk hero of sorts. Young Flowers was a great hurdler—the greatest schoolboy hurdler of his time—owning the fastest times in the nation in the 120-yard and 180-yard hurdles. As a junior in 1964, he set four state records in the AHSAA state track meet and ran the anchor in a state-record winning relay.

As a senior, the 6-foot, 180-pounder was even better. He destroyed the competition, winning everything he tried. When he ran, crowds flocked to watch him. Making him even more intriguing was the fact his father, Richmond Flowers Sr. was the state's attorney general and a bitter political foe of then-popular governor, George C. Wallace. That conflict—and young Richmond's rise to stardom—was later documented in a movie entitled, *Unconquered*, which stirred up tons of controversy and emotion when released in the late 1970s.

The politics of the day had an effect on the younger Richmond. When he won MVP honors at a Southeastern track competition in Mobile, his father was asked to present the MVP medal. Fans stood and booed.

Instead of rattling Richmond, it only made him more determined. Heading into the state meet at Auburn in 1965, the defending big-school state-champion Poets were considered a shoo-in to win a second title.

Coach George "Snoozy" Jones remembers the time well. "We not only had Richmond, but we also had Jack Marsh and some others who made up I think one of the most talented teams ever," said Jones. "But

David "Deuce" Palmer, while at Jackson-Olin in Birmingham.
Courtesy of Birmingham Post-Herald

none was like Richmond. He had such a competitiveness about him, such a determination."

Flowers won the 120-yard low hurdles in a record time of 14.0 seconds. He also won the 180-yard hurdles in 18.9 seconds, and tied the state mark in the 100-yard dash, speeding the distance in 9.9 seconds. His broad jump of 23 feet, 3 inches was also another state record.

He blistered those times during the regular season in 1965. He clocked 13.5 seconds in the 120 hurdles, fastest time in the nation, then ran 18.4 in the 180—which was 2/10ths of a second better than the prep national record.

He also clocked the 100-yard dash in 9.6 seconds, considerably better than his time of the year before.

When the 1965 state meet at Auburn's Cliff Hare Stadium got underway that next spring, Flowers set a new national record with a time of 18.3 in the 180 hurdles prelims. In the finals of the 120 hurdles, he ran 13.8 to win over his own teammate, Mike Patterson. His 9.8 in the 100-yard dash broke the state record he had tied the year before.

More than 6,000 fans were on hand to see this prep legend close out his Alabama prep career in the 180-hurdle finals. When the gun sounded, Richmond was off and running—surging to a 10-yard lead out of the blocks.

Then, quick as lightning, Flowers' drag leg caught a hurdle and sent him spilling to the track as the other runners sped by.

That's when Flowers showed the world the kind of class and determination his track coach had described. He jumped up, scratched and bleeding, and took off running again.

Flowers passed every runner but one—his own teammate Patterson, who won the race in 19.3 seconds.

"I was running real straight up today because I was shooting for the record," he said. "I told my daddy before the race that I would either set a record or fall down. I fell down."

The crowd stood in unison to give him a final salute. And then, Auburn University Director of Athletics Jeff Beard paid him the ultimate tribute when he presented him with the Wilbur H. Hutsell

Trophy as the meet's most outstanding performer for the second year in a row.

"Honors are bestowed for achievement, and Richmond Flowers has accomplished much in this meet," said Beard. "But above all, he demonstrated a brand of courage here this afternoon that is seldom seen on an athletic field or anywhere else."

He earned All-America football honors at Tennessee and was drafted out of college by the Cowboys in 1970. He was a member of Dallas' Super Bowl V team.

Injuries cut his career short.

In 1999, he was named one of the top 25 collegiate receivers of the 20th Century by *Athlon* magazine.

FOR THE LOVE OF THE GAME

If Bobby Humphrey had listened to his mother, he might not have become one of the greatest running backs to come out of the state of Alabama.

Humphrey's run to stardom began with an act of defiance when he went behind his mother's back to play football. "When I started out playing football at Graymont, my mom didn't want me to play," Humphrey said. "I joined the community team without her knowing. She had a rule about being home before dark, and I worked it out where I'd practice during the day and get back home before dark."

Humphrey's scheme worked until his team opened the season. "I was in the eighth grade and we had our first game at Dolomite," Humphrey recalled. "I got in the community van and from Legion Field Dolomite is not just a hop, skip, and jump. Our game was at six o'clock, so it was an evening game, and it was after dark when it ended. I ended up getting three trophies as the MVP for offense, defense, and special teams. Since I had not played football before, the coach put me at defensive tackle, and I led the team in sacks. Then he put me at running back, and the first time I touched the ball I ran 75-80 yards for a touchdown. I ran for another touchdown, and he put me back to return the kickoff, and I returned it for a touchdown."

Humphrey couldn't savor his impressive debut. Night had fallen and he knew his mother would be at home, waiting for him. "I had to figure out how to get back in the house," he said. "I knew I had to face my mama. She was at the door and asked me where I had been. I showed her the three trophies. She figured I loved the game, so she didn't spank me for being disobedient. I was shocked, because if you didn't make it home before dark, there was no legitimate excuse you could give her. That's how I started out playing football."

Humphrey went on to star at Glenn High School in Birmingham. Two games remain etched in his memory, the first during his sophomore season.

"We were playing Walker County, and that's the game I got noticed," Humphrey said. "Walker was one of the powerhouses back then, and we were getting beat pretty bad. We ran a screen play, I caught the ball, reversed field and ran about 75 yards for a touchdown, but it was called back because of a holding penalty. Coach [Wendell] Jones was furious, and out of his frustration, he screamed, 'Run it again.' They moved the ball back 10 yards and I ran in the same direction for another touchdown. I ran 145-150 yards on two straight plays, but only one of them counted.

"Everybody on the Walker County side started cheering, and I got some recognition after that. Someone [from a college] contacted me."

The other memorable game during Humphrey's career occurred during his senior season, and it taught him a valuable lesson.

"I ran for 303 yards against Jones Valley and we lost by two points," Humphrey said. "We didn't have a field goal kicker, so we always went for two. The next day the article read, 'Humphrey runs for 303 yards, but comes up two yards short.' That's because on fourth-and-goal at the end of the game, I got tackled on the 2-yard line. The reason that sticks out is that you can accomplish so many things on the field, but the outcome doesn't show how hard you worked and what you achieved."

Following his standout career at Glenn, Humphrey attended the University of Alabama, where he became the Crimson Tide's all-time leading rusher with 3,420 yards, a mark since broken by Shaun

Alexander of the Seattle Seahawks. He still holds the Alabama single-season record for yards rushing with 1,471, set in 1986.

Humphrey entered the NFL's supplemental draft after his junior season and was selected by the Denver Broncos in 1989. He rushed for more than 1,000 yards his first professional season and was named the AFC Rookie of the Year. He played three seasons with the Broncos, appearing in the 1990 Super Bowl and earning All-Pro honors once. He also played for the Miami Dolphins and Buffalo Bills before his career ended after the 1995 season.

A MAJOR PERFORMER

The wishbone, the "I," the veer and the wing-T were some of the popular offensive formations among high schools in Alabama during the 1970s.

In college at the University of Alabama, Major Ogilvie was a wishbone halfback, but it was the veer that made him a high school star at Mountain Brook. "The veer was suited to my talent," Ogilvie said. "It made it hard to key on any part of our game."

With Ogilvie piling up yards, Mountain Brook won consecutive state championships in 1975 and 1976, finishing unbeaten both seasons. He set a then-state record with 2,504 yards rushing in 1976, his senior season, and was named a high school All-American.

"I had a great time in high school," Ogilvie said. "I was fortunate. We never lost a game my last two years. It doesn't get any better than that.

"My junior year we had a close team. We had only 34 players on the team. We all liked each other. That was a real special team. My senior year we had 75 players. We had a lot of great talent. I had a better year statistically. My junior year we had a great defense, but the offense was more counted on my senior year."

He played under two different coaches those two years—Coach Robert Higginbotham in 1975 and Coach Rick Rhoades in 1976. He credited Higginbotham for preparing him for college under legendary coach Paul "Bear" Bryant.

"Coach Higginbotham was a demanding coach, a taskmaster," Ogilvie said. "He showed me I had to be mentally and physically tough. That got me ready to play for Coach Bryant. Whatever success I had, Coach Higginbotham is one of the folks I can attribute that to."

Higginbotham was equally impressed with Ogilvie as a player. "I don't think a coach could ask for a better player in all aspects," Higginbotham said. "He was not the most talented player I've ever coached, but he was the best player I ever had. He had the desire to be the best. At times, I thought he was working too hard. We would get through with practice and he would still be out there, running on his own. I saw him play hurt. He was the type of guy with the game on the line he would do something to win the game for you."

At Alabama, Ogilvie was an All-SEC performer his junior and senior seasons and played on two national championship teams in 1979 and 1980.

"I learned to enjoy winning in high school," Ogilvie said.

NOTHING RUNS LIKE A CADILLAC

As an assistant coach at Pleasant Grove High School in the early 1980s, Alan Pridmore got to see Bo Jackson up close and personal when Jackson was showcasing the skills at McAdory High in McCalla that would eventually make him a Heisman Trophy winner and a sports icon.

Nearly 20 years later as an assistant coach at Clay-Chalkville High, Pridmore got a close-up view of Carnell "Cadillac" Williams when Williams was displaying the talent at Etowah High in Attalla that would make him the fifth player taken in the 2005 National Football League draft by the Tampa Bay Buccaneers out of Auburn University and the 2005 NFL Rookie of the Year after setting a team record with six 100-yard rushing games, including three to start the season, and finishing with 1,178 yards and six touchdowns on 290 carries.

Pridmore insists that "Cadillac" was a better high school running back than Bo. "He's the best running back I've seen since I've been coaching," Pridmore said. "We could tackle Bo. We couldn't tackle this kid. We played against Bo twice. He always made a play against us.

[Cadillac] had the same kind of ability. He had some running instincts Bo never had. It's not much of a comparison. This boy was a more complete back. He made moves and made people miss, and he was a power runner. Bo might run over you or run around you, but I don't remember him making people miss. I've seen Tony Nathan [from Woodlawn High in Birmingham] and Alan Evans [from Enterprise High], but I've never seen a more complete football player than Williams."

Pridmore would get no argument from Cadillac's high school coach, Raymond Farmer. "I hadn't ever seen a back as good as Carnell," Farmer said. "It got to the point around here that we expected him to score every time he touched the ball."

Williams finished his high school career with 6,537 yards and 92 touchdowns. He had his best season as a junior when he gained 2,627 yards and scored 35 touchdowns to lead Etowah to a state championship in Class 5A.

A personable youngster, Williams was somewhat modest in his assessment of his talents while at Etowah. "I feel I'm elusive and I am able to make folks miss," he said. "I wouldn't say I'm powerful. I give folks different looks. I am a hard, determined runner."

Birmingham sportscaster Mike Raita was so taken with Williams' running style that he nicknamed him "Cadillac." "When he ran, it was almost like he had a second gear," Raita recalled. "He would take a handoff at the 15-yard line and go 85 yards. He was so smooth. On the set one day, we were showing the highlights and we were playing William DeVaughn's song "Be Thankful for What You Got" in the background. I used to sing that song,

"Though you may not drive a great big Cadillac
Diamond in the back, sunroof top
Diggin' the scene
With a gangsta lean
Gangsta whitewalls
TV antennas in the back"

"We only had about 12 or 15 seconds for his highlights, and I just said, 'This kid is so smooth he runs like a Cadillac.'"

2

QUARTERBACKS

STARR SHINES BRIGHT

Bryan Bartlett Starr was a Sidney Lanier back-up quarterback in 1950 when he got his big break—literally.

Backup Poets center Jim Wilson remembered that night. "I was a sophomore, and Bart was a year ahead of me at Sidney Lanier," Wilson recalled. "We were playing Tuscaloosa, and our quarterback broke his leg in the first quarter. Bart went in to play. In the third quarter our center hurt his ankle or knee and came out and I went in. From that time on I played center for the rest of the year, and Bart played quarterback for the rest of the year."

Starr led the Montgomery team to a victory—breaking Tuscaloosa's 17-game winning streak. The win also launched the career of arguably the most successful quarterback in Alabama state history—and it was the beginning of a friendship with Wilson that still thrives today.

"We had a good season," Wilson continued. "That summer Bart went up to Kentucky. Coach [Paul "Bear"] Bryant was at Kentucky and all three of our coaches had played for him—Bill Moseley, Charlie

Bradshaw, and Matt Lair. He went up there and worked out with Coach Bryant and Babe Parilli, the quarterback at Kentucky. When he came back to Lanier, he made All-America as a high school quarterback. He was so far ahead of anybody we played. Bart was fabulous."

Writers in Alabama described Bart Starr as the smoothest prep quarterback in state history. The Poets went 23-3-4 in Wilson's three years. Starr's last season was 1951. He played in and was named MVP of the 1952 North-South prep all-star classic and would then embark on a not-so-glamorous college football career at the University of Alabama from 1952-55. Wilson wound up at Tulane.

It would be in the NFL where Starr would make his mark. He was drafted by the Green Bay Packers in the 17th round in 1956, arguably the best bargain in NFL draft history. Playing under legendary coach Vince Lombardi, Starr guided the Packers to six Western Division titles, five world titles and two Super Bowl victories. He played for Green Bay until retiring in 1971. Six years later, Starr was inducted into the Professional Football Hall of Fame. He served as the Packers' head coach from 1975-1983. In 1976, he was inducted into the Alabama Sports Hall of Fame.

He is proud of his Alabama roots, returning to the state where he is now a successful businessman. He credited his own family for his successes. "I was blessed with a superb father and mother who were team builders and taught great values," Starr said in a 2002 interview. "I have also been richly blessed with a wonderful wife who has uniquely committed to me and was willing to make any sacrifices necessary for my career development."

He also credited the coaches in his life. "Coach Vince Lombardi while we were with the Green Bay Packers was a fabulous leader and inspirational gentleman," said Starr. "I will always be grateful also for the outstanding high school coach, Bill Mosley, we were fortunate to have while at Sidney Lanier in Montgomery. And one of his assistants, Charlie Bradshaw, who later went on to coach at Kentucky, was the best teacher I ever had in the classroom."

HEISMAN BEGINNINGS

Pat Sullivan is well known as the first college football player from Alabama to win the Heisman Trophy, but at John Carroll High School he was known as a pure athlete, starring in three sports. He was an all-state basketball player and a major league prospect as an infielder, and of course, a major college football prospect.

What made Sullivan stand out was his desire. An assistant coach once said Sullivan "fights like a fourth-stringer about to lose his job every day."

He played tailback as a sophomore and switched to quarterback his junior and senior seasons. He was 6 foot 1, 173 pounds. He had approximately 4,000 yards total offense (2,400 passing and 1,600 rushing) as a junior and senior and accounted for more than 350 points, including some as a place-kicker his senior year. He also was the Cavaliers' punter and played defensive back.

"Oh gosh, I remember my high school career being lots of fun," Sullivan said. "John Carroll, when I was coming along, was kind of an underdog. The most we had on the varsity team was 24-28 players. Basically, we played both ways.

"We threw the ball. We ran as much as we threw. We ran the option, sprint-outs and drop back. We ran a good, balanced-type offense. It wasn't like it is today, but sometimes we'd throw it 20-22 times a game. We threw more than other teams. I had some good receivers, Dick Schmaltz, who was a year ahead of me, and David Shelby."

The game that Sullivan remembers the most happened in his final season. "My senior year we were playing Ramsay High School," he said. "It was the first time we played a [Birmingham] city school. They were co-champs of the city championship. It was a big thing in the Catholic community. They had a very good football team, but we were able to beat them.

"Shades Valley and Berry were the big rivals we played every year. The atmosphere was great. My senior year we opened up with Shades Valley, and there were people all around the track. The stadium held 6,000. The people supported it and followed it. It was a fun time in my life."

Pat Sullivan on the run while at John Carroll in Birmingham. *Courtesy of Pat Sullivan*

One road trip, however, wasn't any fun. "We went to Childersburg to play. It was a cold, blustery night," Sullivan recalled. "The football team rode on the school bus with the back window out. The band took two chartered Greyhounds. They stopped and ate at a restaurant. Hugh Craig was our coach and we stopped at a service station. He bought all of us a Hershey candy bar," he said with a laugh.

Sullivan's high school career set the stage for what he accomplished in college at Auburn.

"It doesn't matter what level you play on, you learn to compete and get experience," he said. "No question, playing at John Carroll was a big part of my training. Those were good times. I had success, and that gave me confidence."

Coming out of high school, Sullivan was recruited by several SEC schools, including Alabama, Georgia, Tennessee, and Mississippi State, and also Notre Dame. He chose Auburn, where he became a prolific passer, throwing for 6,284 yards, and won the 1971 Heisman Trophy. When his career ended, he held 24 school records and was responsible for 71 touchdowns (53 passing and 18 rushing), earning a spot in the College Football Hall of Fame. He also played five seasons in the NFL, four with the Atlanta Falcons and one with the Washington Redskins.

TRAMMELL TRIUMPHS

A starter for coach Ed Spears as a freshman in 1954, Pat Trammell went on to become one of the top quarterbacks of his time—some even calling him the best there ever was.

You would've gotten no argument from one Paul "Bear" Bryant.

Trammell, who earned All-State, All-County, All-Southern, and All-America honors in his schoolboy years, was best known as the quarterback who directed Bryant's first national championship team at the University of Alabama in 1961. By the time he reached the Capstone, however, Trammell had already reached legendary status in northeastern Alabama playing at Jackson County High School (Scottsboro) from 1954-58.

To say he was ahead of his time would be an understatement. His first year on the varsity for the Wildcats produced an untypical 3-6-1 record. Jack Cornelius took over as head coach in 1955 and the Trammell-led Wildcats immediately turned things around to 6-3-1. It was his junior season in the fall of 1956 that still has folks talking. They remember the husky tough-as-nails signal-caller who was also known for his basketball and baseball-playing prowess.

Scottsboro went 9-1 and finished tops in the region with only a 25-24 controversial setback to Etowah County of Attalla marring an otherwise 10-0 season. He then started on the basketball team for coach Q.K. "Dusty" Carter that went 36-2 and averaged more than 80 points a game—close to 30 more than the best teams in the state. That basketball season ended on a sour note—more about it in a minute.

Trammell's best football outings came in some of the toughest games. He had a five-touchdown passing night in a 54-7 rout of Oneonta in

1955 and another five-TD passing night versus rival Fort Payne in a 59-6 win in 1956. His two rushing touchdowns and two passing TDs sparked a 40-2 win over Bridgeport in 1956.

Scottsboro closed its season in 1956 with powerful Rossville, Georgia, a much anticipated game in both Alabama and Georgia—so much so that Chattanooga television station WRGP (Channel 3) offered to televise the game on a tape-delayed basis, at that time, a rare recognition for high school football.

Trammell and his backfield mates Bo Davis, Ray Gentles, Cody Hess, and Willard Latham, led the Wildcats to the victory. Fans couldn't wait to see the tape-delayed telecast which was scheduled to be shown at 12:45 p.m.—just after church the following Sunday.

Players and fans alike rushed home from church and clamored in front of the TV sets all across the Tennessee River Valley only to discover the game would not be shown.

As it turned out, the bus carrying the film broke down and did not arrive in Chattanooga in time—leaving Channel 3 barraged with complaints. After several on-air apologies, the game was shown the following Sunday.

Trammell became the object of an intense SEC recruiting battle the next year as a senior. He guided the Wildcats to a 7-3 record, rushing for 18 touchdowns and passing for four on the year. In a time when writing about recruiting was virtually unheard of, Trammell became the subject of a *Birmingham News* Benny Marshall column after he visited Tuscaloosa during the season to take in a game.

He talked later of helping Scottsboro avenge its only loss of 1956 by whipping Etowah in 1957. He rushed for 193 yards on 21 carries and was 5-of-9 passing with two touchdowns in the win. He called that "my greatest game."

Pat Trammell also showed he was willing to help a friend on a tough job. Prior to facing unbeaten and unscored-upon Gadsden later in the season, a teacher work day allowed Trammell and some of his teammates to give up their rare day off from school to help teammates David and Charles Webb pick cotton. The Webb brothers' dad had passed away a few years earlier, leaving the two boys and their mom to run the small farm outside Scottsboro.

Even in the cotton field, Trammell showed his strong competitive spirit—battling teammates to see who could pick the most cotton. Rumor had it that Coach Cornelius won out over Pat as the team helped the Webb boys gather their crop in that single October day.

As for the basketball finish, Scottsboro met Fayette County in the semifinals of the 16-team state tournament at Tuscaloosa with new Alabama head football coach Bryant's prize recruit, Trammell, in the lineup as a high-scoring guard/forward. Fayette County, coached by a former Scottsboro player, held the ball on the high-scoring Wildcats and hit a shot near the buzzer to win 20-18.

The stunned players gathered their composure, then shook the hands of their victorious opponents and reportedly cried all the way back to Scottsboro some three hours away by bus.

Trammell might have been ahead of his time as a player, but his life was also cut short by cancer. After leading Alabama to the national title in 1961 he finished fifth in the Heisman voting. Passing on a professional football career to become a doctor, Trammell died at age 28—a death that saddened an entire state.

THE "SNAKE"

It may have taken the promise of a 1954 Ford to get Kenny Stabler out for football as a ninth grader at Foley High School in 1960. The flamboyant youngster was hooked from day one, however, basking in the limelight as one of the state's first true superstar prep athletes. The left-hander would make his mark in high school as a quarterback and a baseball standout.

It was during those years (1961-63) that he earned the nickname "Snake." The story goes that his coach, Denzel Hollis, after watching Stabler weave through the defense from side to side the entire length of the football field, proclaimed, "That boy runs like a snake."

The nickname not only stuck in high school, it remained with him all the way to college at the University of Alabama and through his entire professional football career.

Back to the car … Snake's dad, Leroy "Slim" Stabler, was quite an athlete himself. The death of his father forced him to turn his own focus from athletics to helping support his brothers and sisters. Slim saw the potential in son Kenny early and didn't want him to suffer his same fate. So he pushed him to be the best he could be.

Word quickly spread across the South about the lanky lefty who was winning football games at Foley, a small-town school located an hour east of Mobile near the Gulf of Mexico.

Stabler led three Foley teams to a combined 29-1 record, including 10-0 in 1961 and 1962, his sophomore and junior years. The only loss of his career was a 20-14 setback to Vigor of Prichard in the first game of his senior season.

In 1963, Stabler completed 64-of-99 passes for 862 yards and 15 touchdowns—school records at the time. He finished his prep career with 24 TD passes and 21 TDs scored. Colleges came calling nationwide.

In 1964, he played in the Alabama High School North-South All-Star game. He also set a school record with 44 points in a basketball game and then turned down a $50,000 bonus to sign with the New York Yankees as a pitcher/first baseman out of high school.

That was the University of Alabama's, and later the NFL's good fortune, however. He chose to play football (and baseball) for Coach Paul "Bear" Bryant.

Bryant considered Stabler to be one of the best quarterbacks ever to play the game—and one of the winningest. He was voted "Quarterback of the Century" at Alabama. He was a member of the 1965 National Championship team and then quarterbacked the 1966 team to a perfect 11-0 season. The '66 National Championship eluded the Tide, however, when Notre Dame and Michigan State chose to play to a 10-10 tie—still the biggest travesty almost 40 years later, according to Tide fans, in college football history.

Stabler quarterbacked Bama to an 8-1-1 season in 1967. The Tide went 28-3-2 record in his three years with Kenny, notching 180 completions in 303 attempts for 2,196 yards, 16 touchdowns, 838 yards rushing, and nine more scores.

He was named the Sugar Bowl MVP in 1967 (a 34-7 rout of Nebraska) and was named the Most Outstanding Back in the SEC by the Atlanta Touchdown Club and Birmingham Monday Morning Quarterback Club in 1967.

The Oakland Raiders drafted him in the second round in 1968—setting in motion an NFL career that ended in 1984. Stabler was named AFC player of the year in 1974 and 1976 and received the Hickok Belt as the NFL player of the year and also won the NFL passing championship in 1976.

Stabler led the Raiders to the Super Bowl XI championship over the Minnesota Vikings, the first Super Bowl title in Oakland history.

He finished with 28,118 yards passing and 194 touchdown tosses in his career, which also took him to Houston and New Orleans.

HOLLOWAY BREAKS BARRIER

When Condredge Holloway became the starting quarterback at Robert E. Lee High School in Huntsville in the late 1960s, few high schools in the state were even integrated. And black high school quarterbacks at predominantly white schools were just unheard of in the South.

Holloway's storied high school career was one for the history books, however. He not only led the Generals to some of their finest football seasons, he also was considered one of the top prep baseball players in all the land. A trailblazer of sorts, he is credited in many ways with helping the state of Alabama move successfully into an integrated high school athletic system.

He was drafted out of high school in 1970 by the Montreal Expos, but chose to sign a football scholarship with the University of Tennessee instead. It would be another decade before a black quarterback would win the starting position at in-state schools Auburn and Alabama, although it took just one year for Holloway to win the starting job in Knoxville.

Called "Miracle Man" in high school for his athleticism and ability to turn bad plays into big gainers, he continued to wear that moniker proudly at Tennessee. So much so that even a song ("Go Holloway") was written in his honor describing his heroics on the football field.

He led the Vols to three straight bowl games (Astro-Bluebonnet, Liberty, and Gator) and a 25-9-2 record as a starter. He had just 12 interceptions in 407 pass attempts (a school record that still stands). He was named Southeastern Conference Sophomore of the Year in 1972 and SEC Junior of the Year in 1973. He also was named MVP of the Hula Bowl college all-star game following the 1974 season (1975 Hula Bowl). He also excelled for the Vols' baseball team, again forcing a choice when he finished in 1975. Condredge was drafted in the fourth round by the Atlanta Braves after hitting .353 as the starting shortstop and earning All-America honors.

He was also drafted in the 12th round by the New England Patriots but opted to go north to the Canadian Football League instead.

The next 13 seasons he rewrote many of the CFL's offensive records while quarterbacking the Ottawa Rough Riders (1975-80), Toronto Argonauts (1981-86) and the British Columbia Lions (1987). Holloway threw for more than 25,000 yards, rushed for 3,167 and was named the league's MVP in 1982. He is a member of the CFL Hall of Fame, and the Argonauts retired his jersey after naming him to the 125th anniversary (1873-1998) team.

He was named the all-time quarterback of the century for UT football.

Holloway is now back at UT where he is an assistant athletic director dealing with player relations. And in Huntsville, he is still the measuring stick for great prep quarterbacks more than 30 years later.

AHEAD OF HIS TIME

On the cover of the September 21, 1964, issue of *Sports Illustrated*, Auburn quarterback Jimmy Sidle was featured with the words: "Year of the Running Back." That was kind of odd because Sidle was a quarterback. In 1963, he became the first quarterback to lead the nation in rushing with 1,006 yards and was named first-team Associated Press All-America. He finished seventh in the Heisman Trophy voting, which was won by Roger Staubach of Navy.

At Banks High school in Birmingham, Sidle also was known more for his strong right arm than his legs. Banks head coach Jimmy Tarrant employed a spread offense with Sidle as his trigger man.

"He was the most outstanding player I ever coached, him and a boy named Bobby Duke at Phillips [High in Birmingham]," Tarrant said. "He could do anything. He had a great arm and he was fast. He was just a good athlete.

"He lived with me one summer. He was a fine boy … just happy go lucky. He'd give you anything he had."

Sidle played at Sylacauga High as a freshman and sophomore, but moved to Banks when his half-brother George "Shorty" White became an assistant coach at Banks under Tarrant.

"Jimmy was way ahead of his time," White said. "He was 6-3 and weighed about 220 pounds. He could be a great player today with his size, speed, and arm. He was the state champ in the hurdles and he could run like a deer. He could really throw the ball. Florida State was throwing the ball and wanted him, but he went to Auburn and they made a running quarterback out of him.

"He's probably the best athlete I've ever been around. He was the starting quarterback at Sylacauga as a sophomore. As a senior, we had lost to Ensley during the season, but we got a second shot at them in the Crippled Children's Clinic, which was like the [Birmingham] city championship. Jimmy put on a show and we beat them.

"He could have gone to college on a basketball scholarship or a track scholarship, but he chose football."

Sidle was the leading candidate for the Heisman in 1964, but injured his shoulder in Auburn's opening game and was moved to tailback. He later played in the NFL with the Dallas Cowboys and the Atlanta Falcons, and in the Canadian Football League.

COAL MINER'S SON

Lloyd Nix grew up right in the middle of coal-mining country in the small community of Carbon Hill. Football kept him out of the mines, enabling him to go to college and become a dentist.

Nix wasn't just any ordinary player. He was a star quarterback at Carbon Hill, but switched to halfback his freshman year in college at Auburn.

"I was a quarterback through high school," Nix said. "When I got to the Alabama All-Star game in Tuscaloosa, Elmore from Athens had Charlie Bolton, his senior quarterback there, and he said, 'Lloyd, I want to put you at right halfback, because Charlie already is familiar with the system, and that way, being left-handed, you can run left and throw left.' When I got to Auburn, they told me they would leave me at halfback, so I could run left and throw left, and we had Tommy Lorino to run right and throw right."

Nix returned to quarterback during his sophomore season at Auburn, calling the move "…the best thing that ever happened to me." Nix led the Tigers to a 10-0 record in 1957 and their only national championship.

At Carbon Hill Nix played for Coach Jack Cornelius. "I think he's the only coach in the state who coached two quarterbacks who led teams to national championships," Nix said. "He coached Pat Trammell at Scottsboro." Trammell led Alabama to a national championship.

Nix directed a balanced attack under Cornelius. "In high school we did it all," Nix said. "We threw a lot and we ran a lot. We were about half and half, passing and running. We ran the straight-T. I played safety on defense."

Nix was surrounded by talented players, but he wasn't considered overly gifted. "During my junior year, our high school team had two ends, two guards, and a fullback who signed with Tennessee," he said. "I should have gone to Tennessee because all my friends were up there. I was recruited by Tennessee, Georgia Tech, Auburn, and Alabama. When I got to Auburn, I remember somebody wrote: 'He can't pass, he can't throw, he just beats you.'"

Carbon Hill finished undefeated in 1953 but didn't get a chance to play for a state championship. "It wasn't set up then like it is now with a playoff system," Nix said. "We wanted to go play Verbena. We couldn't get anybody to set up the game."

Verbena, located in the south central part of the state, was in the midst of a five-year stretch in which it won 50 consecutive games.

"We played teams from Walker County—Jasper, Dora, Cordova, and Oakman," Nix continued. "We used to play a Thanksgiving game in Walker County. We played in it a couple of times while I was at Carbon Hill.

"We also played Pell City. I remember we went to Pell City, and the headline in the newspaper said, 'The Carbon Hill Coal Miners come to town.'" The headline was not flattering and served to fire up Nix and his teammates. "We just killed them," Nix said.

Football brought the townsfolk of Carbon Hill together every time the Bulldogs played. "The atmosphere was absolutely the best," Nix said. "We had about 2,200 folks living in Carbon Hill, and 2,100 were at the ballgames. They followed us everywhere we went."

NATURAL BORN LEADER

By the age of 12, Steadman S. Shealy Jr. was already known to Dothan fans as a player with winning qualitities. The devoutly Christian youngster was a phenom at any sport he tried—especially football, baseball, and basketball.

In a state youth all-star baseball competition, he struck out 18 in a six-inning game. His junior high teams dominated the competition.

Coaches at Dothan High School could barely wait to have him on their varsity teams. "Steadman Shealy was a natural born leader," said former Dothan High head football coach Philip Creel, who inherited Shealy as quarterback in the 1975 season, Creel's first at the helm. "He's a winner. He takes no short cuts. He works hard to excel, and others follow."

In 1974, Shealy led the Tigers, coached by Bobby Sirmon, to the Class 4A state finals at Legion Field—losing 10-7 to Homewood after many on the team grew sick from food poisoning the night before the championship.

As a senior, he led the Tigers back to the finals—this time falling to Mountain Brook and future college friend and teammate Major Ogilvie 29-23. In the finals, the game was aptly called the "Shealy and Ogilvie Show," since both turned in MVP performances.

Shealy led Alabama to its first 12-0 season in 1979 and was named the Birmingham Touchdown Club Player of the Year. He finished 10th overall in the Heisman Trophy balloting. The Tide was 34-2 his final three years.

In high school, Shealy left an amazing record, passing and rushing for almost 2,000 yards as a senior, hit over .500 as a baseball star and earned MVP honors in the Dothan Jaycee Classic 16-team basketball tournament during Christmas.

Legend has it that then-Auburn coach Doug Barfield was sitting in Shealy's parents' house on a recruiting trip that winter while Georgia coach Vince Dooley was waiting outside in his parked car. Shealy's mom came into the living room and interrupted Barfield's visit to tell her son he had a phone call.

"Coach Bryant was on the phone. If it had been anybody else, she wouldn't have interrupted," said Shealy. "He asked me if I was going to sign with him, and all I could think of to say was, 'Yes sir.'"

He quickly became one of Bear's favorite quarterbacks ever—so much so that he spent much time with the Bear and wife Mary Harmon [away from the football field].

Bryant would remark before his death that Shealy had a profound impact on his own life.

They even named a racing greyhound after Shealy, who led Bible studies and FCA meetings in the dorm while in college—attended at times by as many as 100 athletes and other students.

After graduating cum laude from Alabama in 1980, Steadman became a graduate assistant the year Coach Bryant won his 315th game. He assisted on the last Bryant team while he finished a law degree (1984). He even served as host of the *Bear Bryant Show* in 1981. Less than a month after Bryant's final (323rd) win, a victory over Illinois in the 1982 Liberty Bowl, the coach died. Mrs. Bryant asked Shealy to speak at the memorial service at Coleman Coliseum the day after the funeral.

A practicing attorney in Dothan, he married the first female athlete on scholarship at Alabama, former gymnast Ann Wood, and now splits his time between the law practice in Dothan and his family in Tuscaloosa. They have five children.

His daughter Jacqueline Ann is a gymnast at Alabama, and his son Steadman III is a young quarterback at nearby American Christian Academy.

While he left coaching, he did stay active in education—serving on the Alabama State Board of Education from 1986-1994.

A TRUE FIELD GENERAL

The all-time leading passer in Alburn University history is not former Heisman Trophy winner Pat Sullivan or the Washington Redskins' first-round 2005 draft choice, Jason Campbell.

That honor belongs to Stan White, who passed for 8,016 yards during his Auburn career from 1990-93.

White went to Auburn after an outstanding high school career at Berry High School in Birmingham. Legendary Berry coach Berry Finley tabbed White as the Buccaneers' starting quarterback midway through his sophomore season in 1986.

"We started the season 0-4 and had a very talented quarterback who moved [to Birmingham] from the Mobile area," White said. "There was some question about me staying at quarterback and possibly moving to another position. At halftime of the Mountain Brook game [the fifth game of the season], we were behind by two touchdowns. Coach Finley announced that I would be the starting quarterback the second half. We were playing a very talented Mountain Brook team. As fate would have it, we were able to come back and win the game, and I remained starting quarterback for the rest of my high school years."

Finley once said that every coach needs a Stan White at least once in his career. "He's a good one," the late Finley said before the start of

White's junior season. "His most important quality might be leadership. Our players believe in him."

During his senior year in 1988, the 6-foot-3, 185-pound White led an average Berry team to the state championship game. "We started the year with a struggling football team," White recalled. "We lost three out of the first four games, and the rest of the year looked even more difficult. But with the determination of Coach Finley and his staff, we were able to make the 1988 football season one of the most memorable in history. We reeled off nine straight wins to make it to the state championship game and play defending state champs Vigor (of Prichard, near Mobile).

"The semifinal game at Finley Stadium that year was one of the most exciting games that Berry fans and players have ever been a part of. Against a superior team that manhandled us earlier in the year, we were able to come back and score a late touchdown against Minor to go to the state championship game [after a 21-17 victory]. I've played against Alabama four times, I've played at Giants Stadium and in every NFL stadium in the league [at that time], but that game against Minor will always be one of the most precious memories I'll ever have."

White passed for 1,444 yards and 10 touchdowns and rushed for 650 yards and 15 touchdowns during the 1988 season, but he couldn't bring the Bucs a title. They lost 41-7 to Vigor, but White produced the only points against Vigor in five playoff games.

At Auburn, White led the Tigers to an undefeated season (11-0) in 1993, which was their last unbeaten season until 2004, when they were 13-0. He also played four years in the NFL with the New York Giants.

RIVERS CRESTS

When the 1999 football season finally ended for Athens High School following a 33-21 loss to Gadsden in the Class 5A state playoffs, Golden Eagles coach Steve Rivers suddenly realized a big part of his life as he knew it was over. His son Philip had just played his last game for his dad.

Coach Rivers said his son came up to him in the locker room after everyone else was gone, hugged him and said, "Dad, I love you."

Steve Rivers said, "That did it for me. It finally hit me that his playing days for me were finally over."

Philip Rivers had just completed one of the state's most incredible prep careers and a few months later began one of the most storied college careers ever recorded as well.

The 6-foot-5, 212-pound senior finished his final season completing 107-of-195 passes for 2,023 yards and 15 touchdowns. He threw just seven interceptions. He ran 65 times for 323 yards and six touchdowns. On defense at free safety, he led Class 5A with 10 interceptions.

And his team finished 11-2 in '99 and was 23-4 in his two-year tenure as a starter—33-5 in his three years on the varsity. He was chosen permanent captain by his teammates and was named *Birmingham News* state player of the year.

Also a baseball and basketball star at Athens who sported a 3.89 grade-point average, Rivers opted to graduate after the first semester so he could enroll at North Carolina State in January of 2000.

He immediately earned the starting quarterback nod for the Wolfpack in the spring and then went on to a torrid four-year career that included an NCAA-record 51 consecutive starts. Rivers finished with 13,484 passing yards, second in NCAA history, and 13,582 total yards, also second in NCAA history. His 95 career TD passes tied him for fifth all-time and also broke school and Atlantic Coast Conference passing records along the way.

Rivers threw for more than 300 yards 18 times and over 400 yards seven times.

Ironically, his favorite receiver at N.C. State was Jerricho Cotchery, a wide receiver from Phillips High School in Birmingham. The two first met in the state playoffs in Alabama when Athens scored a hard-fought, come-from-behind win over the Red Raiders in '99.

When they closed out their college careers, they left the field together and received a rousing standing ovation.

Phillip Rivers. *Courtesy of AHSAA*

Following that storied college career, Rivers was drafted No. 4 in the first round by the New York Giants in the 2004 draft but was promptly traded to the San Diego Chargers for Eli Manning.

Cotchery wound up with Peter Warrick as one of only two ACC receivers to have 200 catches and 2,000 yards receiving. He finished with 200 catches, 3,119 yards, and 21 TDs and was drafted in the fourth round by the New York Jets.

In high school, Cotchery had 39 catches for 1,008 yards and 13 TDs and made five interceptions on defense. Like Rivers, he also excelled in basketball and was a track standout.

Both Rivers and Cotchery's professional careers were still in full bloom two years later.

"Philip started out coming to the field with me when he was old enough to tote a water bottle and towel," said Coach Rivers, who left Athens following the 1999 season and took a position at a high school in North Carolina so the family could remain close to their son. When Philip moved to San Diego, dad and mom moved to the West Coast to be near their son and daughter-in-law again.

Philip Rivers was a sophomore when his dad left nearby Decatur and took the head coaching job at Athens. Upon arrival, the youngster found himself as a back-up quarterback that sophomore season and a starting linebacker.

Rivers wound up with 3,403 yards passing and 32 touchdowns for his prep career. He also had 14 career rushing touchdowns. On defense, he finished with 17 career interceptions and 203 tackles. A number of colleges wanted him on their side, including Auburn, Ole Miss, and Duke. However, it was North Carolina State that was committed to giving him a real shot at quarterback.

3

DISTINGUISHED COACHES

GLENN DANIEL: ALABAMA'S WINNINGEST COACH

Glenn Daniel recorded 302 prep football coaching victories to become Alabama's all-time leader. He coached eight seasons at Pine Hill High School in central Alabama and then 38 years at Luverne before retiring as a head coach in 1992.

The former A.G. Parrish High School three-sport standout got into coaching, however, literally by accident. Daniel had never thought about coaching as a profession before he left Selma for World War II.

When the war was coming to an end, Daniel was stationed for a brief time in England—along with a member of Adolph Rupp's University of Kentucky basketball team.

"We played a lot of ball together," said Daniel, a standout football, basketball, and baseball player in high school for Coach Comer Sims, who was heading to the University of Georgia before his country called. "He was leaving before me and he told me he was going to tell Coach Rupp about me. And he did."

Once home and out of the military in the summer of 1946, Daniel got a letter from Rupp offering him a chance to be on his team. He went to Lexington and became one of 45 freshmen who tried out for the squad. Daniel was quite a basketball player in high school. At almost 6 foot 4, he helped the high school basketball team start a streak of 88 consecutive regular-season wins. "We went 31-0 and got beat in the state tournament my senior year," said Daniel.

"This was the post-war years, and the players were all much older than the typical freshmen of today. I was 22 and some were older than me. Coach Rupp kept five freshmen," said Daniel. "I was one of the five."

After his freshman year, Daniel, who was married with an expecting wife, came home for the summer and got a call from his former high school coach.

"I went to the Selma YMCA and met with Coach Sims. He told me that Pine Hill High School [30 miles south of Selma] was looking for a new football coach. The man they had hired was killed in a car accident, and Coach asked me to talk to the principal."

Daniel said he was hired to teach a variety of subjects, including history, and became the head football coach for $2,100 the first year.

"I called Coach Rupp and explained that I was taking the job at Pine Hill for one year," said Daniel. "He told me to come back up there in a year." That one year led to eight at Pine Hill, then led to 38 at Luverne.

That first season was quite an experience. "I had zero knowledge about coaching," Daniel said. "I mean nothing. I had never even thought about coaching before I took that job. In high school, I played quarterback in the single wing, which was really a blocking back. Because of my position, I had pretty much learned everybody else's responsibility. So I just tried to do what I knew."

His team scored only two touchdowns that first season. "We beat Dixon Mills 6-0," Daniel recalled. "The first touchdown came against Frisco City and we were down 42-0. The fans would drive their cars up around the field in those days. When we scored, everyone started blowing their horns like we'd won a state championship."

To Daniel, coaching seemed natural. He played semi-pro baseball in the summer and got his degree from Livingston University. "I never made it back to Kentucky," said Daniel. "Those other four freshmen who stayed ended up starting by their senior year."

At Pine Hill, his team went from 1-9 the first year to 4-6, 5-5, 7-3 and finally 10-0 in 1952. The *Birmingham News* named Pine Hill its regional champion. After eight seasons at Pine Hill, Daniel moved to Luverne in nearby Crenshaw County.

"Because I knew nothing, I tried to learn all I could," said Daniel. "I guess I have gone to more coaching clinics than any coach in state history. I took notes and kept them in notebooks. I learned from anybody I could."

Ironically, by the end of his career, Glenn Daniel was the master teacher—sharing his vast knowledge with younger coaches. But he never felt he knew enough. "I still went to coaching clinics," he said. "I loved studying film. One thing I figured out early was that you can always learn something new."

Daniel retired from teaching in 1987—three decades after moving to Luverne. He remained as head coach through 1992—compiling a 302-169-16 record in 46 years as a head coach. His 1991 team won the Class 3A state championship 21-7 over Plainview as more than 5,000 fans squeezed into Glenn Daniel Stadium in Luverne to witness the historic triumph. Former players numbering in the hundreds returned that weekend for a reunion and time of honoring their coach.

Even after retirement Daniel couldn't stay away from the field. He returned as a voluntary assistant coach three years later and helped former player Butch Norman snap Clay County's state-record 55-game winning streak in the 1997. A month later Luverne beat Sand Rock 42-0 to claim the 2A state crown.

He was an advisor to Coach Mike DuBose's 2003 team that reached the state finals. At age 80 in 2005, health problems kept him from the field on a daily basis. He still was serving as an advisor to the coaching staff, however.

"My rules were pretty simple," said Daniel. "I believed a player should never do anything that might bring discredit to his family, school, or team. It was that simple. I only booted a kid off the team as a last resort. I always felt I was there for the kids, not vice versa."

Nationally, only a handful of prep coaches have won more games than Daniel—and even fewer could match his record at one school. At Luverne his teams were 259-132-13 in 38 years—including the 12-3 season in 1991. His last team went 7-3 in 1992.

A true gentleman and leader in every sense, he was selected the Class 3A Coach of the Year and *Birmingham News* state coach of the year twice in the last 10 years of his career. The stadium in Luverne was named for him in 1989. He is a member of the Alabama High School Sports Hall of Fame and also a member of the National High School Sports Hall of Fame.

"I think my biggest weakness was my ability to schedule," Daniel said. "We always played teams much bigger than us. I am sure it cost us another 50 to 100 wins. To me, though, the challenge of trying to beat someone better than you was the bigger learning experience."

EUIL "SNITZ" SNIDER: A WINNER

James "Red" Patton called Coach Euil "Snitz" Snider "a very important person" in his life, although Snider, in Patton's words, "...didn't want any crap from any of his players."

"He was a tyrant as far as working us," said Patton, who played running back on Snider's Bessemer High teams in 1944 and 1945. "He never let any players take a drink of water during practice. He wanted players to conform to the rules. He expected us to go on the field and give 110 percent. He taught us to play hard and mean, but not dirty.

"Snitz was a firm believer in scrimmages and head-on tackle. We'd have a game on Friday, but on Thursday, we had head-on tackle. He'd put half of us on one side and half of us on the other, and we had to run over the guy in front of us."

Despite his unforgiving tactics, Patton described Snider as a "good person" and a "winner." "Like so many coaches, he wanted us to win and he wanted us to be good people," Patton said.

Euil "Snitz" Snider. *Courtesy of AHSAA*

Snider indeed was a winner. He coached all but one of his 32 years at Bessemer, where seven of his teams won state football championships. During his one year at Dora, his teams were county champions in football, basketball, and track. His only football team at Dora in 1929 produced a 6-3-1 record, then he moved to Bessemer, where he was head coach three different times—1933-1940, 1944-1957 and 1960-63. His record at Bessemer was 162-70-12.

Bessemer won because Snider's players were usually in better physical condition than the other the team. "Snitz wasn't a real Xs and Os guy, but he had you in shape," said Jim Ed Mulkin, who played halfback in the Notre Dame Box for Snider in 1947. "He was a great track man and went to the Olympics in track. He ran us to death. He played for the fourth quarter."

A great athlete himself, Snider lettered from 1924 to 1928 in football, basketball, and track at Auburn University. He qualified for the 1928 Olympic Games by setting a national record of 48 seconds flat in the 400 meters. He was the official starter for 25 SEC track meets and 20 Florida Relays. In 1942-43 he was director of the physical education program at Howard College (Samford) and coached the Navy B-12 football team.

As a football coach, "He was kind of all business," Mulkin said. "He wore this felt hat, and if you did something he didn't like, he'd throw it down and stomp on it."

John Vines, an offensive and defensive tackle under Snider for five years in the 1940s, incurred Snider's wrath one day in practice. "I was pulling on a trap play," Vines recalled. "I got tangled up with the offensive guard, and the linebacker came through and crucified the back. Snitz started in on me, and although I knew better, I tried to explain what happened. I told him I got tangled up with the guard and he said, 'Vines, I don't want to hear any excuses. Next time block 'em both.'

"He was a sound, fundamental guy in the Vince Lombardi mold. He was ahead of Bear [Bryant]. He believed if we paid the price, the second half belonged to us."

Snider had a keen eye for talent, sending a dozen of his Bessemer players, including Patton, Vines, and Pro Football Hall of Famer Maxie Baughn to Georgia Tech to play for legendary Yellow Jackets coach Bobby Dodd.

"Phil Tinsley was the first," Vines recalled. "He went over to B-12 training school. Dodd was an assistant and saw what good fundamentals Phil had and then he got to know Snitz. Whenever one of his scouts came over, he told them that if Snitz recommended a player and if they could get in school, to offer them a scholarship. Twelve of us in all went to Tech."

Snider was the first high school coach inducted into the Alabama Sports Hall of Fame, and in 1972 the Bessemer Board of Education named the city's football stadium in his honor.

"I know first-hand of the character he built, the demands he made, the standards and goals he planted in the minds of hundreds of young men, and as you reflect back, you can't help but note the success so many of these former pupils of Snider enjoy in all walks of life," former Bessemer mayor Ed Porter said.

MAJOR BROWN:
DEVOTED TO FUNDAMENTALS

As far as Willie Scoggins is concerned, there was not a better football coach in the state in the 1940s and 1950s than Major Brown.

"Major was a fundamental football coach," said Scoggins, who played quarterback under Brown in the mid-1940s. "He dealt with everything in the game—the kicking game, the passing game, the running game, and blocking schemes. Consequently, his teams were prepared in all phases.

"We had some small players, but they knew how to play. The things you see running backs doing now, we were doing then because Major taught us."

Brown began his educational career at the Negro High School in Decatur in 1934. He stayed there three years as a teacher and head coach before moving to Industrial High School (now Parker) in Birmingham in 1937.

In 1943, he took over as head football coach at Parker and coached the Thundering Herd for 22 years. His 1945-47 teams were undefeated as the Herd put together a 30-game non-losing streak. His teams won more than 120 games and never had a losing season during his time at Parker. He carried eight teams to the Thanksgiving Day TB Bowl in Birmingham, recording seven wins.

"We went all over the state and out of the state, Georgia, Florida, Kentucky to play," Scoggins said. "We'd play anybody who wanted to play. Our 1945 team was undefeated and unscored upon."

Brown demanded excellence and respect from his players. "Major put fear in you," said Scoggins, who went on to become the second-winningest basketball coach in the state. "He did not like for you to make excuses. He'd prefer you just say, 'I made a mistake.' Whenever I did something wrong, I always told him I'd get it right the next time.

"I studied him. He was an unusual guy. He made sure every man knew what they were supposed to do. In practice, he'd go around to every player and ask them what they were supposed to do, and they'd have to tell him.

"I've talked with a lot of guys, and they think Major was ahead of his time."

JOHN EDWARD O'BRIEN: HOT COMMODITY

In the 1940s, J.E. "Hot" O'Brien just might have been the hottest commodity in high school coaching in the Southeast—possibly even the nation.

From 1941 to 1947, O'Brien's Tallassee teams had a 57-game non-losing streak—marred only by one tie.

Writers nationwide were interested in the man known simply as "Hot" at the small school in the Central Alabama town of Tallassee, population 1,091. The Dadeville native was the brother of Alabama's fabled prep basketball coaching legend Mickey "Guy" O'Brien. With

Tallassee coach Hot O'Brien. *Courtesy of AHSAA*

Guy coaching at Geraldine and later Scottsboro and "Hot" coaching at Tallassee, the O'Brien brothers were in a class by themselves.

In Tallassee, boys grew up longing to wear Tallassee's purple and gold. "Many boys who grew up in Tallassee had the privilege of playing football, baseball, or basketball in high school for him," said former player Dr. Daniel P. Wilbanks. "Many more had their spiritual lives enriched through his Sunday School Class at First Baptist Church in Tallassee. I remember when I was just eight or nine he was always stopping by the playground and encouraging us. As a youngster, you couldn't wait to play for him and wear that Tallassee uniform."

O'Brien was more than a high school coach and teacher. He was a community icon. He served as a deacon and trustee at the First Baptist Church and was president of the Tallassee Rotary Club.

He burst on the national scene when the Tigers eclipsed Massillon of Washington, Ohio's 52-game win streak. Massillon, coached by Paul Brown, held the national record at the time.

Born on March 16, 1906, Hot O'Brien was a super athlete at Dadeville in nearby Tallapoosa County before attending Birmingham-Southern College.

Tallassee businessman Davis Melton, another former O'Brien pupil, said the coach was ahead of his time. "Coach Hot O'Brien was a legend in our own time," said Melton. "From 1941 to 1947, he was unbeaten and topped Paul Brown's national record at Massillon [Ohio] of 52 wins in a row. Passing and pitch-outs were unheard of at the time. We had 12 games in a row without giving up a TD and 16 games allowing just six points."

O'Brien compiled a 128-36-7 career record. Through the first 53 games of the 57-game stretch, his teams outscored opponents 1,637 points to 134—or 30.8 points per game to 2.5.

In 1948, his unbeaten team had 116 first downs on the year and the opponents had just 36.

Tallassee's incredible streak began in 1941—a week after Phenix City beat the Tigers 7-0. The next time Tallassee would lose came in the 1947 season. The only blemish on that streak was a tie with Wetumpka in 1944.

After graduating from Birmingham-Southern in 1930, O'Brien became the head coach at Falkville for one year and then went to New Site for a season in 1932. He returned home to Dadeville in 1932 and remained through the 1935 season.

He arrived at Tallassee for the season of 1936—guiding the Tigers to a 7-2 record. In 1937, 1938, and 1939 his teams went 8-1. The 1938 team allowed just eight points all season.

In 1940, the team went 7-2 followed by an 8-1 slate in 1941. The streak started that season on October 10 with a 20-0 win over Eufaula. Tallassee broke Massillon's national record on October 3, 1947, ironically, with a 12-7 win over Eufaula with All-State backs Charles Stough and Billy Stokes leading the way. The 1942 team allowed just six points in the 8-0 campaign. The 1945 team averaged 41.4 points per game and allowed only 25 points in nine games (2.8 points per game).

The 1946 team went to Cramton Bowl in Montgomery and beat Sidney Lanier 12-0—the biggest win in the streak over the state's largest high school at the time.

The most lopsided win was a 72-7 rout of Lineville in 1944. The streak finally came to an end in 1947 when Sidney Lanier beat the Tigers 20-7.

After the 1946 season, fans and boosters got together and bought O'Brien a new Ford car. The Tallassee football stadium was named for him on August 21, 1969, some 23 years later, standing as a testament to the respect this fabled coach received.

In the early 1950s, the University of California was shopping for a head coach, and O'Brien was rumored to be one of the leading candidates. However, the rumors of an offer never bore out, and he remained at Tallassee as head coach through 1952—recording just one losing season in the entire span.

Asking Hot O'Brien to pick his favorite players or favorite team drew consternation from the team-oriented coach. He did say, however, "If I could pick my favorite 33 players for a game, I would fish three days after work and not worry about Friday night."

O'Brien also coached the Tigers' basketball and baseball teams to 11 district titles.

TALLASSEE'S O'BRIEN YEARS				
Year		W-L-T	Pts	Opp
1936	Tallassee	7-2-0	192	50
1937	Tallassee	8-1-0	193	33
1938	Tallassee	8-1-0	236	8
1939	Tallassee	8-1-0	200	39
1940	Tallassee	7-2-0	147	45
1941	Tallassee	8-1-0	169	26
1942	Tallassee	8-0-0	255	6
1943	Tallassee	8-0-0	251	18
1944	Tallassee	8-0-1	284	25
(tie with Wetumpka)				
1945	Tallassee	9-0-0	373	25
1946	Tallassee	9-0-0	251	33
1947	Tallassee	8-1-0	236	65
1948	Tallassee	6-1-2	141	54
1949	Tallassee	4-4-2	96	94
1950	Tallassee	4-6-0	130	127
1951	Tallassee	6-4-0	187	115
1952	Tallassee	4-4-2	170	111
TOTAL		120-30-7	3,511	874

W.C. MAJORS: A SUCCESS IN TWO SPORTS

Pro Football Hall of Famer Lee Roy Jordan grew up in Excel in the 1950s before heading to the University of Alabama and later the Dallas Cowboys. Jordan prizes his high school years. And he cherishes the time he spent with his high school football coach W.C. Majors.

Jordan wrote this comment to members of the AHSAA High School Sports Hall of Fame committee in a successful effort to get his coach enshrined:

"During my career, I was fortunate to have three great coaches— Coach Majors, during my high school career, Coach [Paul] Bryant during my college career and Coach [Tom] Landry during my pro career. I don't think anyone could be that lucky to have three great coaches [like these] in their sports career."

Majors appreciated Jordan's praise. He had another spin on their relationship back in Monroe County in the late 1950s.

"I don't really know if I coached Lee Roy or if he coached me," said Majors. "Lee Roy was a one-of-a-kind player and person. He was a great kid to coach."

Born October 15, 1929, in Frisco City, Majors was a three-sport star for the Whippets, graduating in 1948. He then went to Auburn where he finished in 1953.

His coaching resume included stops at Excel (1955-59), Frisco City, first as an assistant and head basketball coach and later one year as head football coach (1964).

He then began the first of three head-coaching stints at Fairhope in Baldwin County—where he compiled a 110-30-1 record from 1964-70, 1973-75 and finally, 1981-85. He spent one year, 1975-76 coaching at Monroe Academy. His teams combined were 153-46-3 in football and 151-41 in basketball.

Few coaches had the combined success he had in both sports. His football teams won 21 in a row at Fairhope and went 57-3-1 in one stretch. His teams went to the state playoffs 10 times and his 1974 team played at Mobile's Ladd Stadium in the Shrine Bowl.

Majors was named state football coach of the year in 1972. He was South all-star basketball coach twice (1960-64).

He saw 80 players sign football scholarships with 40 signing with Division I-A major colleges. Two, Jordan and Randy Rockwell, served as captains of the team at the University of Alabama. Another, David King, had a stellar career at Auburn.

Highly thought of statewide, Majors was on the AHSAA committee to set up the state playoffs for football in the 1960s.

The stadium at Fairhope was named in his honor—a stadium that has served as a practice site for some of the top NFL future stars in history while the players were in Mobile preparing for the annual Senior Bowl.

JAMES GLOVER: "GENTLEMAN JIM"

It took Robert Higginbotham only one season to discover that James "Gentleman" Glover was a special coach.

"Coach Glover hired me right out of college to be his defensive coordinator," Higginbotham said. "I didn't realize the tradition they had. They would pour concrete slabs and put the years they won state championships on them. He was one of the legends from the state."

Glover began his career fresh out of Delta State College in 1940 at Brookwood High School in Tuscaloosa County and produced an 8-7-1 record in two seasons. He spent the next three and a half years in the United States Navy, working with boxing great Jim Tunney in a service physical fitness program.

After World War II, Glover went to Jefferson County High School (now Tarrant) for three years before moving in 1947 to Etowah County High in Attalla, where his reputation became legendary.

He coached for 31 years at Etowah. He was 194-96-15 with six undefeated teams and a state championship. His teams played in Gadsden's Charity Bowl game 24 times. He had a 35-game winning streak, and during one five-year span, his teams went 48-2.

Overall, he finished with a record of 213-110-16.

"He won his 200th game the year I was there," Higginbotham said. "He showed me that it takes a good work ethic to be successful. He did a great job of on-the-field coaching, and he was great at motivating his players.

"I remember the night before a game the team would go to a restaurant downtown and bring in some of his old players and let them talk. He could get a team as emotionally ready for a game as anyone."

Glover also was a demanding coach and a disciplinarian. "I remember one time the best player on the team had gotten into trouble and it took him a long time to get back into Coach Glover's good graces," Higginbotham recalled. "He had the other players line the field five yards apart and the boy had to run through every one of them. All was forgotten after [the punishment]."

Of Glover's former players, 73 went on to play college football, and 36 became coaches. Eleven became ministers, eight high school principals, and six college professors.

When he retired after the 1977 season, Hootie Ingram, then-assistant commissioner of the Southeastern Conference, said: "I don't know what they're planning to do for him, but in my opinion the entire state should give him the biggest tribute in sports history. He's done more for high school football in Alabama than anyone I know."

In 1978, the Attalla Stadium was renamed in Glover's honor. He had personally sold $63,000 worth of the $90,000 in bonds sold to build the stadium, which seated 8,500 people, more than the population of the city at that time.

Glover received several coach of the year awards and in 1985 was inducted into the Alabama Sports Hall of Fame.

HAYWOOD "BIG TRAIN" SCISSUM: AN INNOVATOR AND MOTIVATOR

Cecil Leonard looks at all the pass-happy offenses that are now in vogue and recalls his days of playing high school football in the early 1960s under Coach Haywood "Big Train" Scissum at East Highland in Sylacauga.

Scissum coached for 18 years at East Highland, and his teams were noted for their explosive offense, often averaging more than 40 points per game. His 1969 team was unbeaten (9-0) and scored 499 points, while giving up only six, a lone touchdown scored by the other team's defense.

"He was way ahead of his time," said Leonard, who played quarterback for Scissum from 1961-63. "The man had a heck of a football mind. He knew how to stop you and how to beat you with offense. We did things back then that people are doing now to win. We ran the spread offense and the shotgun. It wasn't whether we would win, but how many points we'd beat you by. They used to call me 'Bad News,' and one of the officials would say to me before the game, 'Bad 're not playing but a half tonight because of how many points we are going to score.'

"Coach Scissum was an innovator and motivator. He knew how to get the best out of his players. He used to challenge us, especially when we were playing what was supposed to be a tough opponent. He'd say certain things to make you play harder. I remember one time he sent a boy in from the sidelines and he said, 'Coach Scissum said run the football if you aren't scared.' He knew that would make me mad and more determined.

"Everybody in Sylacauga wanted to play for him."

When Leonard was head coach at Parker High in Birmingham in the 1980s, he said he incorporated many of the schemes Scissum used when he played for him. "A lot of the stuff we did at Parker I learned from Coach Scissum, such as the double-wing formation," Leonard said. "I just refined some of it."

Scissum's teams won two state championships and finished as runners-up once, while compiling an overall record of 135-29-11. He

East Highland coach Haywood Scissum (left) receives a plaque honoring him. *Courtesy of AHSAA*

had three undefeated seasons and only one losing season. In the 1960s, Scissum had a 34-game winning streak.

In the years before the state's black and white athletic associations merged, Scissum's East Highland teams won the North Eastern Interscholastic Athletic Association district football championship nine times in 18 years, and he was the District Coach of the Year nine times.

Former Scottsboro district attorney Dwight Duke, who went to East Highland as a young white basketball coach in 1968, said Scissum should not only be judged for how many games he won, but for turning boys into men.

"Scissum was more than a coach to these boys, many of whom were fatherless, many were the sole supporters of their family," Duke said. "He instilled in them pride, a burning desire to achieve, and the determination to overcome any obstacle placed in their path."

Following his successful tenure at East Highland, Scissum went to Tuskegee Institute (now Tuskegee University), where he compiled a 66-48-1 record.

HIGGINBOTHAMS: LIKE FATHER, LIKE SON

Robert Higginbotham laughed when talking about playing high school football under his dad and coach Morris Higginbotham. "It was pretty tough playing for him," Higginbotham said. "He expected a lot and demanded a lot."

Morris Higginbotham also won a lot. During the first nine years of his coaching career at three different schools, he won six state championships named by the *Birmingham News*. In a career that began in 1952 and spanned more than 30 years, he coached at seven high schools, including Walnut Grove, West Blocton, B.B. Comer in Sylacauga, Enterprise, Hueytown, Hewitt-Trussville, and Scottsboro. He also had three-year stint at Livingston State College (now the University of West Alabama).

He influenced several of his former players to become coaches, including his son, Robert. "My dad gave me the foundation and starting point that was invaluable," Robert Higginbotham said. "He worked extremely hard and showed me how to get the very best out of everyone's ability."

Robert Higginbotham also has enjoyed a successful coaching career, posting a 245-118-3 record through 2005 while coaching three years at Mountain Brook, 23 years at Shades Valley in Birmingham, and seven years at Tuscaloosa County. He won a state championship at Mountain Brook in 1975 and finished as runner-up twice at Shades Valley.

"I got a lot of my coaching philosophy from my dad," Robert Higginbotham said. "He showed me that you have to pay attention to the little things, and that expectations were very important. You have got to expect to do well because kids pick up on that."

In 1993, Morris Higginbotham was inducted into the Alabama High School Sports of Fame, and Robert Higginbotham joined him in 2002, becoming the first father-son pair in the hall of fame, a feat Robert Higginbotham called "the most thrilling moment" of his career.

ANDERSONS: DEANS OF COACHES

Dovey Anderson never wanted his sons, Charlie and Buddy, to become coaches, although he was very successful in the profession.

Anderson spent 31 years coaching football (and other sports) in his hometown at Thomasville High School, beginning in 1931. His career record was 182-81-25, and his teams outscored their opponents by a better than 2-to-1 margin, shutting out almost half of the opposition. Three of his teams finished undefeated, and seven others had only one loss.

When he retired in 1962, a newspaper article described him as the "dean of Alabama high school coaches."

"He wasn't ready to retire," Buddy Anderson said of his dad. "He had told Charlie and me that he never wanted to coach either one of us, because he never wanted to be put in a position of folks saying he treated us as favorites. So when my brother went out for football, he retired."

After Dovey Anderson retired, Thomasville had a steady stream of coaches. "I played under four different football coaches in four years,"

Buddy Anderson said. "Any time you change, and I'm not saying change isn't good, everything changes. You have different offenses and different defenses, and what coaches are looking for is different.

"I also played under three different basketball coaches and three different baseball coaches. I remember one night after a basketball game—it was January 12, 1968, I can remember it like it was yesterday—I was frustrated with the situation, and the frustration had come to a head. I was sitting in my truck, it was overcast and a storm was about to come by. I cried out to God, 'Why is all this happening?' That's one of the few times God spoke to me, not audibly, but through my heart. He told me He wanted me to be a coach, a Christian coach. That's what my dad was, and I had witnessed his rapport with his players."

Buddy Anderson went home and told his dad about his decision to become a coach. His dad didn't want to hear it. "He tried every way he could to talk me out of it," Buddy said. "He had already talked my brother out it, and he would have been a better coach than me.

"Finally, he said, 'Since I can't talk you out of it, let me give you some advice.' I told him I wanted to major in physical education and he said, 'Don't be a P.E. teacher, because there are so many coaches I know who are P.E. and history teachers.' So I minored in math and most of my career I taught math."

Buddy Anderson began his coaching career as an assistant at Vestavia Hills High in 1972. He took over as the school's head football coach in 1978 and is the dean of football coaches in the Birmingham area. He has a record of 232-100 in 28 seasons (through 2005) and has won two state championships and been runner-up twice.

He was inducted into the Alabama High School Sports Hall of Fame in 2003, joining his father, who was part of the first induction class in 1991.

"That's the most humbling thing ... to be in there together with my dad," Buddy Anderson said. "The plaque I have in there is right next to his."

BOB FINLEY: R-E-S-P-E-C-T

During his football career, Mike Kolen had the pleasure of playing for two Hall of Fame head coaches. At Auburn, he was a two-time All-SEC linebacker in 1968 and '69 under Coach Ralph "Shug" Jordan, a member of the College Football Hall of Fame, and in the pros he played eight seasons for the Miami Dolphins, including their perfect season in 1972, for Don Shula, a member of the Pro Football Hall of Fame.

But one of the coaches he always admired was Bob Finley, who was a young assistant at Berry High School in Birmingham when Kolen played there in the mid-1960s.

"Normally, Coach Finley would go out and scout the next week's opponent," Kolen recalled. "He'd come back with a scouting report that was two inches thick. His scouting reports were thicker than the ones provided to me in pro football. It was obvious he paid attention to detail. I knew he had a bright future by the way he approached the game.

"He had a real care and concern for his players and their lives and future. They wanted to perform for him. He was truly a player's coach."

Finley coached 27 of his 30 years at Berry. He took over as head football coach in 1968, and his 23 football teams posted a record of 179-79-5 with two state championships (1977 and 1982) and two second-place finishes (1969 and 1988) in 12 playoff appearances. He also had a successful tenure coaching Berry's girls' basketball team, taking them to four Final Four appearances in eight years.

Finley was respected by his peers, and in 1984 headed the list of Birmingham's Most Respected High School Football Coaches. After receiving the honor, Finley compared his coaching philosophy to that of former UCLA basketball coach John Wooden. "I don't look at wins and losses," Finley said. "Yes, I hate to lose as much as anyone. But I take John Wooden's description of success. He said success is bringing people to maturity … helping mold young men so they can make a positive contribution to society."

Finley died unexpectedly on July 31, 1994, just after cutting the grass on the Berry football field that bore his name.

Berry coach Bob Finley. *Courtesy of AHSAA*

In a commentary about Finley's death, radio personality Ben Cook said, "He sent a lot of football players on to college scholarships, but he sent a lot more young people into life. The football players were ready for college football because Bob Finley was a great football coach. The young people were ready for life because Bob Finley was a great man."

NOLAN ATKINS: A MASTER OF MOTIVATION

When Sweet Water coach Nolan Atkins took his Bulldogs north from Marengo County in 1986 to play powerful Courtland in the Class 1A state championship game, he had his team stop in Birmingham for a lunch break.

He picked up a copy of *The Birmingham News* and noticed the predictions about the championship games scheduled later that night. His team, a decided underdog, was picked to upset the Chiefs.

"After our kids got back on the bus, I told them that big-city sports writers know their stuff," said Atkins, who became one of Alabama's st successful high school football coaches during his 30-plus years as a prep coach. "And I told them how we had been picked to win.

"That was the motivation we needed. To be honest, I didn't see how our small team could play with their big, fast players.

"Doggone it, they did. We went out that night and won the game 26-14."

It was on a small football field known only as Victory Field that he created a monster power in small school football in Alabama. Atkins directed Sweet Water to four state titles en route to his 229-57-3 record at the school. He also coached the baseball team to a 130-40 record and six state titles in a 12-year span (1979, 1980, 1982, 1983, 1986, 1988, and 1989).

Atkins grew up in Columbus, Mississippi, attended Lee High School there and later Mississippi State. In 1966 he moved across the state line to Sweet Water while his twin brother Roland was just up the road at Thomaston. Roland coached Marengo County (Thomaston) to the AHSAA's first-ever Class 1A state title in 1967 when the state playoffs were opened to every school in the AHSAA. Marengo County drubbed Valley Head 42-7 in the finals.

By 1969, Nolan Atkins had his own team in the finals—losing 30-6 to Excel.

Before he was through, Sweet Water had reached the finals seven times with championships in 1978, 1979, 1982, 1986, and runner-up teams in 1969, 1975, and 1984.

He might have won even more except that Sweet Water was closed in 1981 with Nolan moving over to Thomasville. The community demanded the high school be reopened, and Atkins returned to win a state title the next year.

Nolan Atkins admittedly was old school when it came to football. His teams were famous for the wing-T, fullback-oriented offenses and tough-as-nails defenses. His players were a collection of country boys— white and black. His success at integrating the team in the late 1960s and early 1970s was a rare success story as communities all around him deserted the public schools for private academies.

Sweet Water coach Nolan Atkins is carried off the field by his players. *Courtesy of AHSAA*

;ins retired from Sweet Water in 1991, finishing his career with a 278-78-5 record. In 2003, the stadium was named in his honor and is now called Atkins Stadium/Victory Field.

As for that stop in Birmingham in 1986, he said, "We had a bunch of kids who just wouldn't give up."

Atkins coached at least one player who reached the NFL (Randy Beverly) and another who reached the majors in baseball (Cedric Landrum). His quarterback Michael Landrum became the first black quarterback signed by coach Paul "Bear" Bryant at the University of Alabama. Several of his former students went on to coach, including Stacy Luker, who guided Sweet Water to the 2004 state title with another Landrum, freshman Anthony, scoring four touchdowns in a 35-7 win over a heavily favored R.A. Hubbard team from none other than Courtland.

"I found my niche at Sweet Water," Atkins said. "It was a great place to teach, coach, and raise a family. I guess that's why I still live here."

SPENCE McCRACKEN:
HE DIDN'T LISTEN TO HIS MOM

Spence McCracken loved playing high school football at Robert E. Lee High School in Montgomery in the 1960s. And he relished his time at Auburn University from 1968-1971.

When his playing days were finally over, his mother gave him some practical advice. "She told me to get a real job, and she begged me not to go into coaching," said McCracken.

He took his mom's advice—at first. He went to work for Spartan Foods, known in layman's terms as Hardee's Hamburgers. He worked at the district level for more than a year. That's when he remembered the other part of his mom's advice. "She told me to do something I enjoyed doing," he said. "So I went into coaching."

McCracken began his coaching career at Decatur, Georgia, as an assistant in 1973. He returned to Montgomery the following year and was an assistant football and head track coach at his alma mater Lee

High School from 1974-1978. When Montgomery Academy needed a head football coach, he jumped at the chance to get some experience.

And in 2006, after 251 career wins, Spence McCracken is still having a ball going to work each day. "My mother wanted me to have a career where I could make some money," said McCracken. "I preach to my players all the time for them to listen to their parents. But I also tell them they have to stand up and make good choices. My mother raised me right."

McCracken is considered one of the top prep coaches in Alabama. After four years at Montgomery Academy, he went back to Lee as head football coach and took the program to the top of the nation over the next 11 years.

His 1992 team was ranked No. 1 in the nation for a while and finished No. 2. He has been named national coach of the year and has produced such outstanding players as Fred Beasley (Auburn and San Francisco 49ers); Anthony Brown (Auburn), Larry Ware (Georgia), Tyrone Rogers (Alabama State and Cleveland Browns), Cory Larkins (Tennessee), Melvin Oliver (LSU), T.J. Jackson (Auburn), and Will Herring (Auburn) to name a few.

He guided Lee to three state championships (1986, 1991 and 1992) before heading to Opelika in 1995. His overall 251-71-1 record includes 98-31-1 at Opelika. His 2005 Bulldogs team reached the 6A semifinals.

McCracken, who was one of the youngest coaches to be inducted into the AHSAA Sports Hall of Fame when he was included in the Class of 2004, has been a vocal ambassador for his chosen profession.

"Coaching is a great job, I mean a great job," he said. "Kids haven't changed all that much through the years, but I think the parents have. I think I am happiest when we are practicing. I love the game, and I love the interaction with the kids."

He has promised to retire from coaching in 2008, but first he would like to take Opelika to its first state championship.

"Your goal is to win. That's why you play the game," he said. "It teaches you so much about yourself and about life. The real mark I think of a coach's career isn't his wins, but the impact he has on the

Opelika coach Spence McCracken talks to his players. *Courtesy of Amanda Ingram*

young people he coaches. I can promise you this. Coaches had a major impact on my life when I was growing up. I just hope that I've had some impact on the kids' lives in the same positive way."

LARRY GINN:
FOOTBALL IS ALL IN THE FAMILY

Alexandria High School and the Ginn family are like two peas in a pod. And the legend of "Death Valley" is interwoven into this family's history.

First, Larry Ginn, the head football and basketball coach since 1986, was a star quarterback in the 1960s. A talented passer and runner, he was named to the All-Southern Team along with such standouts in the state as Johnny Musso and future Heisman Trophy winner Pat Sullivan. Ginn went on to Jacksonville State, where he starred in basketball.

When he got out of college, his hometown and his old coach Lou Scales beckoned him back. Ginn has been there ever since.

"I grew up here," said Ginn, who served as an assistant to Scales for 13 seasons. "My sons played for me here, my dad played here. My wife is involved. It's a family thing for us for sure."

The devout family man is just the second head football coach at Alexandria in the last 58 years. Scales coached there from 1948-85. He compiled a 224-145-15 record during that span and won the 4A state championship with Ginn as his assistant in 1985.

Scales retired after that season; Ginn was the natural man to replace him. Since then, Alexandria has risen to even greater success—winning state football titles in 1995 and 1997 as Ginn compiled a 183-53-0 football record over 20 seasons from 1986-2005. His teams regularly go deep in the playoffs. Ginn became perhaps the only head coach in state prep history to guide teams to the state basketball and football championships in the same year (1998).

Ginn was in his 36th year as a coach at the school in 2005. His sons Todd, Scott, and Will have all played quarterback for their dad. And each has had a hand in either a football or basketball championship or both.

Todd directed the Valley Cubs to the 1995 state title. Scott guided Alexandria to the 1997 championship, and Will was 12-1 as a senior in 2002. Combined, the brothers passed for more than 10,000 yards and 100 touchdowns between them.

When Alexandria hosted its 50th anniversary at Lou Scales Stadium in 2002, hordes of past players paraded back to "Death Valley." Scales and Ginn combined have gone 407-198-15 over the last 57 years. Two head coaches in that long span is just unheard of in the modern climate of coaches coming and going.

Scales' last team beat Elba and another 200-game winner, Mack Wood, in the 1985 finals at Death Valley. Ginn's last football championship came at Birmingham's Legion Field in the 1997 Super

Six championships. Scott Ginn was the starting quarterback. Mr. Football that season, Mac Campbell was the starting tailback.

"Mac's senior season is one of the most satisfying to me," said Ginn. "He had a great high school career, but after our last game in 1996, he got deathly sick [with meningitis]. He not only came back, but he came back and had a great senior season."

The Valley Cubs were 39-2 from 1995-97—the best stretch in the school's successful football history.

In 1995, Todd Ginn quarterbacked Alexandria to the state championship as a junior. The next year as a senior he earned MVP honors as the Valley Cubs won the 1997 4A state basketball championship with his brother and first cousin on the same team.

Later that summer, Larry Ginn, who played in the 1968 North-South All-Star basketball game, coached his son in the Alabama-Mississippi All-Star basketball classic at Florence. He coached in the Alabama-Mississippi All-Star football classic in Mobile the next summer.

"I think we've had a real special relationship through the years," said Larry Ginn. "I have always tried to emphasize more important things than winning. I tried to treat Todd [and my other sons] like my other players when it came to coaching. My goal with all my players is to help them learn how to be good fathers some day. If I don't do that, I haven't been successful, no matter how many championships we win."

Ginn said coaching his sons has been a major highlight of his long coaching career. All got their starts as managers when they were still in grade school.

"I've heard some coaches say they don't want to coach their own kids in high school," said Larry Ginn following the 1997 basketball season. "As far as I'm concerned, they're missing out on a real treat. You ought to be coaching them at home in the right way to live, so it seems only natural to coach them in sports, too."

Winning the state championship is the ultimate goal for a Ginn-coached team each season—whether it be basketball or football. "Everybody ought to be able to experience this feeling once in a lifetime," Ginn told a press conference full of reporters following the

'97 football championship. "I don't know why anybody would want to take a drug or alcohol, because this is the greatest feeling you can experience."

SHORTY, PEA SOUP AND SNAKE EYE

Alabama's long-running tradition of outstanding high school football coaches goes as far back as the game itself. And with the colorful tradition comes some colorful men who wore their title of "Coach" proudly.

Among them were H.L. "Shorty" Ogle, Hugh "Pea Soup" O'Shields, and Aubrey "Snake Eye" Hicks. All three are members of the AHSAA Sports Hall of Fame—and all three established traditions at their respective schools that are still flourishing in 2006.

Aubrey "Snake Eye" Hicks he spent more than 30 years coaching high school football or serving as an administrator. All but four of those years were at Addison in Winston County. He compiled a 143-47-7 record during his 18-year head-coaching stretch with the Bulldogs.

He later served in administration and was a leader statewide serving on various committees, including the AHSAA Central Board of Control and was president of the AHSAA coaches association.

Hicks, who grew up in Phenix City, had the stadium at Addison named in his honor. The 2005 Addison team—which included sons of fathers who played on Hicks' 1970 state championship team—went 14-1 and won the 1A state crown. His nickname, it seems, came from his younger days when rolling "snake eyes" was a favorite pastime of young soldiers serving their country.

Hugh "Pea Soup" O'Shields the Geraldine High School and Jacksonville State graduate, picked up his nickname in high school where he was a football star and track standout. Small in stature, "Pea Soup" could run the 100-yard dash in fewer than 10 seconds.

O'Shields compiled a 245-67-12 record with state championships at Oneonta in 1971 and 1972. He coached 17 years at Cleveland in Blount County and then 15 years at Oneonta.

O'Shields had five unbeaten teams. He retired after 1984 at the age of 56.

Oneonta's Redskins program continued to flourish thanks to O'Shields' solid foundation. Oneonta won the 2004 state 3A championship at Legion Field and was second in the state in 2003.

H.L. "Shorty" Ogle, legendary Decatur head football coach, was the Red Raiders' boss from 1933 to 1963. His teams went 8-1 in each of the 1939, 1940, and 1941 seasons. All three losses were to Huntsville.

A key player for Ogle those three years was Bud Lee, a big lineman who would go down as one of Shorty's favorites through the years. A strict disciplinarian, Ogle eased his rigid practice rules for Lee—who went to work in the local Coca-Cola plant following his dad's sudden death prior to his senior year.

Lee became the bread winner for his family, practicing only on Thursdays and then suiting up for the Red Raiders on Friday nights. No player disagreed with Ogle's decision. Instead, they all marveled at his kindness and understanding.

The football stadium in Decatur is named for Ogle.

"I bet Coach Ogle never had a player he let do that besides Bud," Bob Sittason, a former teammate and longtime friend of Lee's, told the *Decatur Daily*. "Coach knew of Bud's financial difficulties. He knew Bud would've had to drop out of school if he couldn't arrange Bud's schedule so he could go to work."

In 1939, Decatur shut out every team but Huntsville—losing to the Crimson Panthers 13-0.

A highlight of Ogle's 1940 team came against unbeaten and unscored-on Athens in 1940. More than 4,000 showed up to see Decatur win 16-7.

In 1941, Ogle worked secretly with his team on the newfangled "T" formation that was being used by Stanford University and the Chicago Bears. After two wins, Huntsville beat Decatur 7-6 as Ogle stuck to his Notre Dame Box offense. Four more wins set up a final meeting with Huntsville on the road at Goldsmith-Shiffman Stadium.

Decatur led 7-6 at halftime when the players begged their coach to let them run the "T" formation in the second half. The second half is

Coach Snake Eye Hicks. *Courtesy of AHSAA*

one that legends are made of. The Red Raiders reeled off 40 unanswered points and won in a rout, 47-6. Legend has it that with that surprise tactic, Decatur became the first high school football team in America to employ the "T" formation in a game.

The following week, Decatur finished 8-1 with a 40-0 win over Hartselle—outscoring opponents 316-20 that season.

Ogle stood 6-4 in high school at Albertville, so his buddies called him "Shorty." The nickname stuck. A starter in all sports, he attended Birmingham-Southern where he was an All-Southern end for coach Red Drew. He also lettered at BSC in basketball, baseball, and track and was awarded the Porter Cup signifying him as the best athlete in the school.

His coaching career began at Hanceville in 1929. He left for Decatur four years later for a lucrative $100 per month. His teams won 33 straight at one stretch at Decatur, and he had four undefeated teams that were declared state champions.

His career record was 253-73-9 in football, 232-42 in basketball, 128-29 in baseball, and 147-31 in track. Among the players he coached were Admiral Don Whitmire, who was a University of Alabama All-American and NFL Hall of Famer, and Auburn all-star quarterback and coach Bobby Freeman.

He is also called the "Father of the Alabama All-Star Game," coaching the North to a 33-0 win in the inaugural North-South.

In 1979, Ogle was inducted into the Alabama Sports Hall of Fame.

Hugh O'Shields. *Courtesy of AHSAA*

4

FAMILY TIES

GOODES: ALABAMA'S FIRST FAMILY OF FOOTBALL

I f ever there was a "first family" of Alabama high school football, it would have to be the Goode boys from Town Creek.

Dad Clyde Goode Jr. was a college football star, and his brother Aaron was a college hurdles champion. Both handed down their athletic abilities to their children.

Clyde, who coached in Lawrence Country at Courtland and later served as principal at nearby Colbert County High School and Hazlewood High School, fathered four sons—Kerry, Chris, Pierre, and Clyde III. He also raised his sister's son, Antonio Langham.

All five played collegiately at Alabama, and all five played on state championship teams at Hazlewood of Town Creek—a city of slightly more than 1,200 in Lawrence County in north-central Alabama just 40 miles south of the Tennessee border.

The Goode connection was one legends are all about. The Goode family lived in the shadows of the end zone of the football stadium at

Hazlewood. When Poppa Clyde went jogging in his younger years, his sons would fall in behind—prompting a merchant at a local gas station to say: "It looked like a big duck with all its little ducks running down the road."

The Golden Bears' football tradition goes back to their first state championship in 1970 when Hazlewood beat Ohatchee 44-0 for the Class 1A title. Aaron Goode, who became the head football coach 35 years later, was a running back on that team.

Another title came in Class 2A in 1975 with another rout, 53-0 over Hokes Bluff in the finals. In 1978, The Bears lost in the finals to Elmore County 7-6.

Clyde Goode's boys first suited up at Hazlewood in the late 1970s with Chris Goode the first. By 1981, he was such a standout running back that he captured the *Decatur Daily* Player of the Year award as Hazlewood won the 1981 Class 1A title. In 1982, brother Kerry was the *Decatur Daily*'s player of the year as the Bears won the 2A state crown, and in 1983 and 1985, the Decatur newspaper's proud honor went to third brother Pierre. During that span from 1980-85, Hazlewood was 64-4.

"It is pretty amazing when I think about it," said father Clyde. "Looking back, I think each of my boys had their own contributions. We didn't think our kids were any different than anyone else. They all worked hard to be the best they could be."

Chris and Kerry headed off to college as Pierre stormed onto the scene in '83. By the time he was a senior, Pierre had become the fastest school boy in state history—clocking 10.39 in the 100 meters to set a state record that lasted until 1999.

Pierre also set state marks in the 300-meter hurdles (38.64), and the 110-meter hurdles (13.73), a record still standing in 2006.

Pierre was also named Mr. Football in 1985 after rushing for a state-record 85 touchdowns and scoring a state-record 233 points in his senior season. He closed out an incredible senior season by scoring all his team's points in a 23-16 win over Autaugaville in the state finals.

Like Chris and Kerry, Pierre also attended Alabama—but not before handing down the torch to his younger brother Clyde III and his cousin, Antonio Langham. The torch may have unofficially passed when Antonio was a freshman.

In an 80-0 rout of region foe Red Bay, Pierre had five carries for almost 200 yards and four touchdowns in the first half. The Bears then subbed in ninth grade-backup Antonio, and he closed out with four carries for 188 yards and four scores.

Hazlewood won 2A state championships in 1985, 1988, 1989, 1990, 1991, 1992, and finished second in 1993 and 1994.

In 1989, Antonio had four interceptions in a 75-0 win over Georgiana in the 2A finals. In 1988, he scored the game's final 10 points with five seconds remaining in the fourth quarter and in overtime in a wild 17-14 come-from-behind OT win over Cordova in the semifinals.

Antonio and Clyde III also attended Alabama.

By 2000, Clyde Jr. had a grandson, Chris Jr., playing at Hazlewood. He helped the Golden Bears claim the 1A state title with a 23-16 win over Reeltown in the Super 6 finals at Legion Field. Chris Jr. was named MVP of that championship game.

All had their bright moments in college. Kerry had 297 all-purpose yards, including a kickoff return for a TD versus Boston College in 1984 in just over a half before suffering a knee injury that ended his season in 1984.

Pierre returned a kickoff 100 yards for a score in one game, and Antonio was a star of Bama's SEC championship game win over Florida in 1992.

Clyde's saw three of his four sons and his nephew Antonio all play in the NFL. Chris spent seven years with the Indianapolis Colts. Kerry played with the Denver Broncos before another knee injury cut his playing career short. He then spent more than a decade serving as a strength and conditioning coach for his pro boss Dan Reeves, first at Denver and later with the New York Giants. Pierre played one year at Denver and then had stints in the CFL and Arena Football.

Antonio came out of Bama as a first-round draft pick of the Browns and spent seven seasons in the NFL. He had 14 career interceptions, including five in 1996 for the Baltimore Ravens.

Poppa Clyde turned down a chance at pro football to go to work out of college and raise his family.

SINGTONS: SETTING A HIGH STANDARD

Fred Sington II knew little about the high school football career of his father, Fred Sington I, other than he played at Phillips High in Birmingham in the mid-1920s and two of his teammates were Ben Chapman, who became more renowned as a baseball player, and Chink Lott, who became a highly successful high school football coach.

"He talked about how he played on a pretty good high school team and they had pretty bad equipment," Sington II said. "But he talked more about his high school baseball career and more about Alabama."

Sington I was a two-time All-America tackle on both sides of the ball at Alabama from 1928-1930. He helped the Crimson Tide win a national championship in 1930. He received national acclaim when Rudy Vallee dedicated his song "Football Freddie" in honor of the Tide star. A Phi Beta Kappa student, Sington was called the "greatest lineman in the country" by Notre Dame coach Knute Rockne. Sington later was named to the College Football Hall of Fame and the Alabama Sports Hall of Fame.

So, when Sington II arrived at Ramsay High in Birmingham in the mid-1950s, he already had a famous name and was expected to live up to the standards his father had set on the gridiron.

"He was a great player," Sington II said. "Everybody was comparing me to my dad. The pressure was always there, but you learn how to deal with it. My dad didn't put any pressure on me. He tried to take the pressure off. He was a big influence on me. He believed there was only one way to play and you trained to do it right, and he also taught us that if you start something, you finish it."

Sington I didn't get to see his son play much at Ramsay, because he was a Southeastern Conference football official. He saw more of his other son, Dave, who was two years younger than Sington II and became an All-State offensive tackle at Shades Valley in Birmingham. Dave drew comparisons to his older brother.

"With the Sington name, we were always compared to each other," Sington II said. "I was compared to my dad, and David was compared to me."

The highlight of Sington II's career was playing in three consecutive Crippled Children's Classics on Thanksgiving Day, which was sort of a bowl game for the best two teams in Birmingham.

Both Sington II and Dave went on to play at Alabama in the late 1950s, but neither had the kind of college career their dad did.

Sington II's son, Fred Sington III, however, came along in the 1980s and won a state championship with Gadsden High in 1986 and a NCAA Division II national championship with Troy State in 1987 as an offensive lineman and punter.

NEIGHBORS: PIPELINE TO ALABAMA

As a boy growing up in Tuscaloosa, Billy Neighbors used to listen to Washington Redskins football games on the radio. His favorite player was Harry Gilmer, who had been a legendary triple-threat quarterback at Alabama in the 1940s.

Late one summer, Neighbors' dad Sidney took young Billy and his older brother Sid Jr. on a cross-country train ride to California, where the Redskins were in training camp, to watch Gilmer practice.

"They used to practice at Pepperdine University," Billy Neighbors said. "When I saw Gilmer and the Redskins practice, I was hooked on football."

Football was already in Neighbors' blood. His dad had played at Tuscaloosa High School in the late 1920s for legendary coach Paul Burnum and was a teammate of John Henry "Flash" Suther, who became an All-America running back at Alabama in 1930.

"My dad played when Tuscaloosa High never lost a game," Billy Neighbors said. "I think he was a lineman. He was on that team when they caught a train to Chicago and beat a team up there and claimed they won the national championship."

In 1926, Tuscaloosa indeed beat Senn High of Chicago 42-0 and boasted they had won the mythical high school national championship.

Sidney Neighbors Sr. had a scholarship to attend Alabama, but because of the Great Depression, he had to go to work instead.

Sid Jr. and Billy Neighbors both became star football players at Tuscaloosa County High School in Northport and went to Alabama. Sid lettered in 1956 and 1957 but was kicked off the team before his senior season in 1958 by first-year Crimson Tide coach Paul "Bear" Bryant for being a few pounds overweight, Billy Neighbors said.

Billy Neighbors was part of Bryant's first recruiting class and became an All-America tackle on offense and defense. He helped the Crimson Tide win the 1961 national championship, played several years in the American Football League with the Boston Patriots and finally was inducted into the College Football Hall of Fame in 2003.

Billy's two sons, Wes and Keith, turned out to be star football players too, at Huntsville High School. "No doubt they were going to be football players because they had been around it all their lives," Billy Neighbors said.

Wes was one of the top college prospects in the nation and rated ahead of Bo Jackson as the top prospect in the state in 1981 when he graduated and later became a two-time All-America center at Alabama in the mid-1980s. Keith played linebacker and lettered at Alabama only one year (1990) because of injuries.

THE CROYLES: BRODIE AND JOHN

It is rare when a high school football standout becomes known statewide by his first name. It is even rarer for a father and son to earn that distinction of fan recognition.

John Croyle and his son Brodie did just that in prep careers that were more than 30 years apart. Both were destined for greatness—though taking much different routes.

First, John was a defensive end and tight end as well as a basketball star at Gadsden High School in the late 1960s—playing in the state basketball finals in 1968. At Alabama, he was a two-sport star as well, but knee problems began to take their toll by the end of his college career.

Still, the All-America defensive standout was able to play on a national championship team at Alabama in 1973 and SEC championship teams in 1971 and 1972.

Selected second-team All-America at defensive end, he was looking a career in the NFL in the eye when he went to coach Paul "Bear" Bryant seeking some advice. He told his coach of his dream of creating a ranch for homeless boys—creating an environment of hope for the kids considered "lost causes" by so many. He also told Bryant of his chances of playing in the NFL.

Now one of the nation's most dynamic speakers, he has retold the story time and time again.

"Coach, if I go to the pros and play four or five years, I can probably make enough money to start the boys' ranch," he said. "What do you think, Coach?"

Bryant then gave him a bit of advice that has touched the lives of thousands of kids helped through John and Theresa Croyle's Big Oak Ranch.

"John, don't ever do anything you don't totally believe in. Don't do anything you aren't totally dedicated to. You believe in that dream of yours. Forget the pros. Go build the ranch. John, if you do that, I'll do everything I can to help you."

Bryant was true to his word. So were many of his former college teammates, such as John Hannah, who have donated time and money to make the Big Oak Ranch a reality.

The ranch is where John and Tee raised their two children, son Brodie and daughter Reagan. Reagan went on to play college basketball at Alabama and was crowned homecoming queen before marrying another Tide quarterback, John David Phillips. Both went to work at the ranch.

John's dream for his "kids" was to provide a Christian education, so his ranch purchased former Westminster Christian Academy in Rainbow City and renamed it Westbrook Christian. He helped coach the football team, and his wife taught at the school.

As an eighth grader, Brodie burst onto the Alabama prep scene as a talented quarterback—leading the Warriors to the Class 1A state finals in 1997. Before his prep career was over, he rewrote the state record books, becoming the all-time career prep passing leader with 9,323 yards on 524-of-997 pass completions. His 105 TD passes were also a record. And he did this despite missing all but one quarter of his senior year. He broke a leg in the season opener and sat out the remainder of the season.

Heading into his senior year at Westbrook in 2000, Brodie had already set the state record for hitting (.672) in 1999 as a shortstop and pitcher. He also set the state single-game passing record with 528 yards versus Donoho in 1998 as a sophomore and the state single-season record for yards (3,787) and TD passes (44) the same season.

He enrolled early at the University of Alabama in January of 2001 and was named the recipient of the Ozzie Newsone Most Improved Freshman award in spring training. He became the starter by his red-shirt freshman year in 2002.

Playing quarterback at Alabama in perhaps the most volatile time in school history, Brodie started 39 games including 12 games as a redshirt freshman. Injuries plagued his otherwise spectacular college career. He finished with 6,382 yards passing and 41 TDs with just 22 interceptions, despite having a revolving door of head coaches and offensive coordinators.

By the end of his college career in 2005, the 6-foot-3, 205-pound Croyle was the Crimson Tide's all-time passing yardage leader. He also owned career marks for completions (488), attempts (869) and touchdown passes (41). He also had the satisfaction of leading Bama out of a probation era with 10 wins his senior season.

More importantly, he remained true to his faith and his upbringing and became one of the most popular players in Crimson Tide history.

He and his dad and his dad's ministry have been the focus of television specials on CBS, NBC's *Today* and ESPN.

Brodie has graced the cover of *Sports Illustrated*, and he was a finalist for the Johnny Unitas Award and a semifinalist for the Davey Bryan Award. He was also selected the SEC's Most Valuable Player at midseason by *SI* and was named national player of the week by the Walter Camp Foundation after his stunning play in the Tide's upset of Florida in 2005.

The son calls his dad the "man I most admire." And he calls his parents' ministry, now the Big Oak Boys and Girls Ranch, an integral part of his roots.

"Growing up there made me anything and everything I am today," Brodie said as he was leaving high school and reiterated time and time again throughout his college career. "I see the work my dad and mom have done, and it makes me very proud. I know the situations a lot of them [the ranch boys and girls] come from.

"I am the lucky one. I have a wonderful family. Our family is on display every day. Dad tells me it isn't enough to be a good football player and good kid at school. He tells me you have to be a Christian example all the time. I wouldn't trade any of this for the world."

And neither did his dad.

RUTLEDGES: GROOMED TO BE ATHLETES

Jack Rutledge wasn't interested in his sons, Gary and Jeff, becoming outdoorsmen, although in Alabama that was one of the favorite pastimes for fathers and sons.

"My dad was a tremendous athlete," Gary said. "He went to Talladega High School and was All-State in football and baseball. He went to Alabama to play football in college, but he converted to baseball and played for four years. He went to the pros and made it to Triple-A with the [Chicago] Cubs. He never could get to the big leagues, then I was born, so he gave it up.

"He groomed me and Jeff to be athletes. We can't hunt or fish or change the oil in a car, but we could play just about any sport.

"He groomed me to be a baseball player more so than Jeff, but my junior year at Banks [High in Birmingham], I had calcium deposits and couldn't play baseball, and my senior year I broke my leg. I had a football scholarship to Alabama, so that's what I did, but I think I was better at baseball than football."

Gary played quarterback at Banks in the late 1960s. "I had a good high school football career, but there were only four schools that could go to the playoffs, so I never got to the playoffs," he said. "We ran the veer style option; and when I got to Alabama, they switched to the wishbone, which was the perfect offense for me."

Jeff Rutledge was four and a half years younger than Gary and also was a quarterback. He didn't mind following in his brother's footsteps. "That didn't bother me," Jeff said. "He was my role model; he was my hero. I didn't start playing quarterback until the eighth grade. Gary didn't start until he was in high school. Being able to follow him was an honor."

Jeff was All-State at Banks and helped the Jets win state championships in 1972 and '73. He also attended Alabama and wore his brother's Crimson Tide jersey number. "When I went to Alabama, I wanted to be No. 11 because that was Gary's number," Jeff said.

Gary guided the Tide to a national championship in 1973, and Jeff did likewise in 1978.

"A guy did a portrait of Gary and me [in 2005], and he told us we were the only two brothers who won national championships at the same school while playing quarterback," Jeff said. "I think that's neat."

GARGISES: A REAL FAMILY AFFAIR

In the early 1970s at Colbert County High in Leighton, the football team was overrun with players named Gargis.

"My senior year we had six or seven starters named Gargis, including myself," said Phil Gargis, who was the team's quarterback. "There was my cousin Alan Gargis at offensive tackle and my cousin Thomas at guard, and my cousin Ricky on the defensive side. Heck, I can't think of all of them."

During Gargis' sophomore season, his older brother David was his teammate and a senior quarterback. But just before the season started, David hurt his ankle, and Phil took over as quarterback. When David returned from his injury, he moved to running back and receiver.

With so many Gargis guys on the team, it might have been difficult for Colbert County head coach C.T. Manley to single out the right one when he made a mistake, but Phil said that wasn't the case. "When we messed up, we knew which one he was talking to," he said with a laugh.

Phil Gargis led Colbert County to the state playoffs his junior and senior seasons, teaming with pro football Hall of Fame tight end Ozzie Newsome and former University of Alabama receiver Thad Flanagan to bring the Indians a state championship in 1972.

"We were a close-knit group," Phil said. "We lived about six or eight miles outside of town in the country in Ford City. We didn't ride the bus to school. We had a hand-me-down car and when we drove in, there'd be about eight or 10 us riding to school together. And every day before a game, we met at somebody's house. It was a great experience."

Phil went on to play quarterback at Auburn University and later settled in Homewood, a suburb of Birmingham, where his sons, Phillip Jr. and Parker, excelled as quarterbacks.

Phillip was brought up to the varsity late during his freshman season in 1995; and although he didn't get to play in the playoffs, he received a state championship ring after Homewood won the Class 5A title. He went to Auburn after he finished high school, but never lettered.

Parker led Homewood to state championships in 2000 and 2002 and a runner-up finish in 2001. He's now a reserve quarterback at nearby Samford University.

"They both had a lot more skills than I did," Phil said. "Being brought up around football gave them a good knowledge of the game, and I'm sure that gave them a boost."

CASTILLES:
FOOTBALL BECOMES A WAY OF LIFE

Little did Jeremiah Castille know that he was starting a football factory when he began playing at Central High in Phenix City. His intention was to just find a way to get a college education.

"Playing high school football was a great experience for me," Castille said, "but I didn't play just for the enjoyment of it. I played because I wanted to do something with my life. I had a chance to fulfill one of my dreams of getting a college education, and I did that when I got a scholarship to the University of Alabama."

Castille's superb senior season earned him that scholarship, but he also has fond memories of how the Red Devils put together a winning season. "My senior year we weren't expected to win any ballgames," Castille said, "but five or six guys came together and we said we wanted to prove everybody wrong. We won seven ballgames and got beat in the first round of the playoffs in 1978."

Castille went on to become an All-America defensive back at Alabama and played several years in the NFL with the Denver Broncos and Tampa Bay Buccaneers.

He and his wife, Lori Jean, also had six children, including sons Timothy, Simeon, and Caleb. Castille wouldn't let his sons play football until they were in the sixth grade, but once on the gridiron they became naturals. Tim started on the varsity as a wide receiver in the eighth grade at Briarwood Christian in north Shelby County. By the time he ended his high school career in 2002, he had established a state record (since broken) for all-purpose yards, 9,544, and scored 102 touchdowns. He helped Briarwood win two state championships and became a prep All-American before signing with Alabama as a running back.

Simeon also played at Briarwood, including three seasons as a teammate of his brother, and became an All-America defensive back his senior year, recording 60 tackles and nine interceptions (two were returned for touchdowns) and helping Briarwood win another state championship in 2003. He also signed with Alabama.

Jeremiah never envisioned his sons becoming star football players. "When they were small, I didn't see them as football players," Castille said. "I didn't put a lot of emphasis on it. I probably discouraged it more than encouraged it.

"Then Tim started getting big as a teenager, and I started seeing some of his athleticism and he had some physical tools. Simeon developed a little later than Tim, but I started noticing his athleticism, and I told myself those guys have got some talent to play at the next level."

Caleb was set to enter his freshman year at Briarwood in the fall of 2006. "We've got to wait and see how he turns out," Jeremiah Castille said.

RASHEEDS: AS GOOD AS THEY COME

In more than 30 years as a high school football coach, Robert Higginbotham has coached his share of siblings, but there's one set of brothers who stand out above the rest—the Rasheeds. Anwar, Dawud and Saleem Rasheed played for Higginbotham throughout the 1990s at Shades Valley in Birmingham.

"It's every coach's dream for a family to come along like that," Higginbotham said. "They had a sister, too, who was an outstanding athlete. They were great, great kids. The thing that is so unique about them is they were raised by their mom by herself, and they were always dressed to the 'T' and they were all very smart students.

"They were Muslims and there were times they would fast, but you never noticed a thing when they were playing athletics.

"Anwar, the older brother, may have been the toughest. He was a 175-pound defensive end, and he was always going up against guys bigger than him. Dawud was just under 6 feet and was a three-year starter. Up until his senior year, he played offense and defense, but his senior year he played mostly offense."

A fullback-linebacker, Dawud responded to just playing in the backfield his senior year by rushing for 1,816 yards and scoring 28 touchdowns, He was named the state's 1994 "Mr. Football" and led the

Mounties into the '94 Class 6A championship game, but they lost to Anniston. Dawud played college football at Duke.

Saleem, the youngest, was the biggest and best of the Rasheeds. A 6-2, 220-pound linebacker, he was the No. 1 college prospect in the state his senior year in 1998.

"I knew he would be good from watching him in the eighth grade at Gresham [Middle School]," Higginbotham said. "When he got up to [Shades Valley], watching him for a couple of days of practice, he was better than I thought. He started for us as a ninth grader and was our leading tackler. I knew he was going to have a bright future."

Saleem led the Mounties in tackles in each of his four seasons, including 157 his senior year, when he also had 12 sacks and 32 tackles for losses. "He's the best linebacker I've ever coached," Higginbotham said.

Saleem became an All-SEC linebacker at Alabama and was a third-round selection of the San Francisco 49ers in the 2002 NFL draft.

"They made so many big plays for us at Shades Valley," Higginbotham said. "It was a real thrill to coach all of those kids. I've always wished another family would come along like that one."

JONES: COACH DAD

For Joey Jones, being around his sons, Joe Jr. and Jake, while they were growing up was priceless, and coaching them was a bonus.

Jones didn't have a dad around during his teenage years as he grew up in Mobile. His parents had divorced when he was seven. Three years later, at the age of 10, he was watching a NFL Monday night football game with his dad when his dad collapsed and died of a heart attack in front of him.

Joey Jones went into a shell. "I was real withdrawn after the divorce and that," Jones said. "It was tough. It was the kind of thing where you ask yourself, 'Why am I going through this?'"

Jones' mother eventually remarried when Jones was 13, but Jones said his stepfather "was a drunk," who once put a gun to Jones' forehead, threatening to shoot him. His mother also drank, making his teenage years even more difficult.

He needed an escape, an out, and found it in football. Jones developed into a 5-foot-9 receiver with blazing speed and good hands. He was timed at 4.2 seconds in the 40-yard dash. "A lot of what happened in my childhood helped me become a better football player," Jones said. "All the anger and hostility I had carried over to football."

Jones played at Murphy High School in Mobile for Coach Robert Shaw, who became a mentor. "He was an innovator when it came to throwing the football," Jones said. "He had a great mind for the game. He knew the technical part of the game. He was way ahead of his time."

Jones' speed and pass-catching ability earned him a football scholarship to the University of Alabama, where he played from 1980-83. The first three seasons of his college career he played for legendary Coach Paul William "Bear" Bryant.

Jones was a second-team All-Southeastern Conference receiver his senior season at Alabama, and that led to a brief professional career. He played two years for the Birmingham Stallions in the defunct USFL and two years with the Atlanta Falcons in the NFL. After his playing career ended, Jones went into coaching, spending time as a volunteer assistant under Coach Terry Bowden at Samford University and as an assistant under Coach Fred Yancey at Briarwood Christian School before landing his first head coaching job at Dora. He also got married, and he and wife Elise started a family. In addition to Joe Jr. and Jake, Jones has a daughter, Caroline.

Jones completed his 10th season at Mountain Brook in 2005 and has a 125-36 record in 13 years as a head coach overall, including 104-27 with the Spartans. Although he coached both of his sons at Mountain Brook, he didn't insist that they become football players. They gravitated to the sport because of their dad's involvement.

"From the time they were four or five years old, I could tell they wanted to play football," Jones said. "I remember 'Joe Joe' wearing a Chicago Bears outfit and Jake wearing a Cincinnati Bengals uniform. I think he liked the stripes on the helmet. They just developed a love for football growing up. Certainly being exposed to it early had something to do with it."

Jones' sons, who could pass for twins despite their two-year age difference, were playing football in the seventh and ninth grades at Briarwood when he decided to move them to Mountain Brook. Jones didn't want any scheduling conflicts on Friday nights with his games and his sons' games.

"It wasn't bad over there," Jones said. "I'd go watch them play on Thursday night or Tuesday night, but as they started getting older, I couldn't fathom not watching them play. So I talked to my wife and we found a house in Mountain Brook."

Joe Jr. played his first season under his dad in 2001 as a sophomore. "Playing for my dad is different, but not many people go through it," Joe Jr. said. "I don't feel that much pressure playing for him. I don't get nervous or anything. Football has been a big part of his life. He loves it, but he balances football and being a dad."

Joe Jr. developed into an All-State receiver under his dad and plays football for nearby Samford University. Jake became an All-State defensive back and signed a football scholarship with Alabama on February 1, 2006.

Jones cherished coaching his sons and being active in their lives. "It was special," he said.

Joe Jr. enjoyed playing for his dad and likes how dad made sure he spent time with his sons. "That's one of the things I admire him for," Joe Jr. said. "It's amazing how he grew up without a father. It makes me more appreciative. It's pretty moving."

5

DYNASTIES

TUSCALOOSA BLACK BEARS (1925-1931)

Before and after he served as the state's 37th governor from 1923-27, William "Plain Bill" Brandon was probate judge in Tuscaloosa County. He also was president of the Tuscaloosa Chamber of Commerce in 1927 and '28 and later, in a Chamber publication, described what Tuscaloosa was like in the 1920s.

"Tuscaloosa roared in the '20s," Brandon wrote. "You could hear us all over Alabama and from coast to coast. ... And, by golly, we showed everybody that our little 'ole country boys who talked funny could also play football. Tuscaloosa High School won the national championship in '26 when it skunked Senn High of Chicago 42-0. That was a mythical title because there were no such rankings. But we claimed it just the same. The THS Black Bears had seven straight perfect seasons, '25 to '31, something like 65 games in a row. Coach Paul Burnum might've been elected governor, but I'm glad he didn't run. 'Cause I did."

Burnum was the architect of the Black Bears' dynasty, coaching them from 1925-29 before leaving to become freshman coach at Alabama. During his five years at the helm, Tuscaloosa played 45 games and won 44. The only blot was a 7-7 tie with Cullman in '25. Burnum's teams outscored their opponents 1,926 to 100. The '29 team did not allow a single point until the final game of the regular season, a 20-6 victory over Bessemer. The Black Bears also claimed mythical national championships in 1926, 1927, 1928, and 1929 by winning four postseason intersectional games—42-0 over Senn High of Chicago in '26, 33-7 over Lakeland, Florida, in '27, 19-6 over McKinley Tech of Washington, D.C., in '28 and 18-12 over University City High of St. Louis in '29.

"As far as I know, no other team in this state or any other state ever did anything like that," said Buck Hughes, who played on all four of those teams and was an All-State halfback in '28-29.

Not everyone gave Burnum full credit for Tuscaloosa's streak. Author William Bradford Huie attributed the Black Bears' success to its connection to the University of Alabama football program. In a 1941 article in *Colliers Weekly Magazine* entitled "How to Keep Football Stars in College," Huie, who attended Alabama and worked there, wrote:

"The Tuscaloosa High School squad was a most important incubator in the Tide hatchery. During the years I was at the university it was coached by Paul Burnum, who is noted for thoroughness in teaching those twin fundamentals, blocking and tackling. It was generally understood that at least part of his salary was paid by the university. He

Most Consecutive Games without a Loss (includes ties)		
Games	School (Record)	Years
64	Tuscaloosa (61-0-3)	1925-1931
58	Andalusia (57-0-1)	1972-1978
56	Tallassee (55-0-1)	1941-1947
55	Clay County (55-0-0)	1994-1997
50	Verbena (50-0-0)	1950-1954

romoted to freshman coach, and his rivals will tell you cleverest recruiting agents in the business. ...

couldn't take full credit for his great high school squads which usually won the state championship. For he was assisted by other Alabama scouts. Suppose a scout found a good prospect who could play another year or two in high school. And suppose the prospect had a poor coach who didn't teach the Alabama system and who might try to recruit the prospect for a competitor. The scout simply picked up the prospect and brought him to Tuscaloosa High School, where he could play on a championship team and where Burnum could start teaching him the Alabama system."

But even after Burnum left Tuscaloosa to join the Crimson Tide coaching staff, the Black Bears continued to win, going undefeated in 1930 and 1931, to finish their seven-year run with a record of 61-0-3, a state-record 64 consecutive games without a loss.

LEE-MONTGOMERY GENERALS
(1955-1965, 1969-1970, 1986-1992)

Perhaps no new school had the type of success that the Robert E. Lee Generals of Montgomery enjoyed after it opened in 1955 as a branch off of Sidney Lanier. Coach John T. "Tom" Jones' teams were so dominant that former Lee principal Clinton Carter called the period from 1955-1965 the "Tom Jones Era" in Alabama high school football.

Jones coached Lee's first team ever to a 6-4-0 record in 1955. The following year, the Generals were undefeated, one of four such teams Jones would have, and one of 10 consecutive teams that would finish in the final top 10 in newspaper polls.

Jones won or shared state 4A championships in 1958, 1959, 1960, 1962, and 1963. His 1958 team was the unanimous champion in all four of the media polls conducted that year. When he left Lee after the 1965 season, Jones had compiled a record of 95-12-5.

"His coaching was marked by intelligence and intensity, which gave impetus to success," Carter said.

"He had one of the finest offensive minds I have seen in all of my years of football experience," said Jim Chafin, an assistant under Jones and later the Generals' head coach.

Jones' departure didn't signal the end of the Generals' success. In 1966, Lee, featuring wide receiver Terry Beasley, was ranked No. 1 in the state in Class 4A (when there were only four classifications) until losing to Sidney Lanier 10-0 in the final game of the regular season. Lee got another crack at Lanier in the championship game in the first year of the state playoff system, but came up short again, falling 9-7 before a crowd of more than 25,000 at Cramton Bowl in Montgomery.

Three years later, Chafin guided the Generals to the 1969 Class 4A title with a 28-13 against Woodlawn of Birmingham, and in 1970 they repeated thanks to an influx of players from Booker T. Washington, which had reached the 1969 semifinals, but was closed because of integration. A few of the more talented players who wound up at Lee from Booker T. Washington were running back Ralph Stokes, defensive back Mike Washington, and end George Pugh. They helped Lee go undefeated and beat Minor of Birmingham 27-7 in the Class 4A championship game.

Following the 1970 season, the Generals had a long drought between championships. Then, in 1984, Spence McCracken, who had played at Lee in the 1960s under Chafin and had been an assistant coach there, returned to his alma mater as head coach. "When I went back, I wanted to instill the tradition that Lee had under Coach Jones and Coach Chafin," McCracken said.

During his 11 years as Lee's head coach, McCracken posted a 118-25 record, won state championships in 1986, 1991, and 1992 and produced such players as running back Larry Ware, the state's Mr. Football in 1986, and fullback Fred Beasley, who played several seasons in the NFL, primarily with the San Francisco 49ers. McCracken's 1986 team was 15-0 and was ranked second nationally by *USA Today*, and he was named national coach of the year.

Coach Jim Chafin guided Robert E. Lee-Montgomery to back-to-back state championships in 1969 and 1970. *Courtesy of AHSAA*

SIDNEY LANIER POETS (1957-1968)

Bobby Wilson had a distinguished football career as a player, especially in college at the University of Alabama, where in 1953 he was Captain of the Crimson Tide's 1953 Orange Bowl championship team. He also ranked third in the nation in punting that season, and he ended his collegiate career as a member of the College All-Stars that played the Detroit Lions at Soldier Field in Chicago.

But what he did as head football coach of the Sidney Lanier Poets was even more remarkable. He arrived at Lanier in 1956 as an assistant, moved up to head coach the next year and turned the Poets into a dynasty. During his 13 years at the helm, the Poets won six state championships and compiled a 92-24-6 record.

Lanier's first three titles—in 1957, 1961, and 1964—were determined in various newspaper polls throughout the state, but the next three—1966, '67, and '68—were decided on the field, representing the first three years of Alabama High School Athletic Association state playoff system.

The first title under the playoff system came during one of the memorable games in the history of high school football in the state. The Poets defeated the Robert E. Lee Generals, their neighboring rival, 9-7, in what was described as the "biggest sports event" ever held in Montgomery.

The Generals had been ranked No. 1 all season and the Poets had been No. 2, but Lanier defeated Lee 10-0 in the final game of the regular season 10-0 in the rain before a crowd of 25,000 at Cramton Bowl. Randy Moore kicked a 33-yard field goal in the second quarter, and quarterback Mike Kelly passed 5 yards to Jimmy Rhodes for a touchdown in the third quarter.

Both teams advanced to the playoffs and easily won their semifinal games with Sidney Lanier clobbering Shades Valley of Birmingham 47-7 and Lee thrashing Huntsville 46-7.

Their rematch attracted more than 25,000 fans, and the game was broadcast live on TV by WSFA in Montgomery.

Lanier scored nine points in the first half, but late in the third quarter Lee scored a touchdown to cut the Poets' lead to 9-7. The touchdown was set up by a spectacular catch by receiver Terry Beasley, who later teamed with Heisman Trophy quarterback Pat Sullivan at Auburn to form the university's most prolific passing duo ever.

In the fourth quarter, the Generals drove inside the Poets' 5-yard line, but a disputed interception by Lanier's Greg Carr on a deflected pass ended the threat and sealed Lanier's 1966 championship.

ANDALUSIA BULLDOGS (1972-78)

When Bill Anthony joined Andalusia's varsity football team as a sophomore tight end in 1976, the team already had put together three consecutive undefeated regular seasons. But Anthony said he and the other newcomers didn't feel any pressure to keep the streak going. "We had watched it, and we were just anxious to be a part of the varsity," Anthony said. "I had watched my brother play two years before I got up there."

Anthony's brother, David, was Andalusia's starting quarterback as a senior in 1976, and with little brother aboard they helped the Bulldogs reach the Class 3A championship game. They battled Athens to a 7-7 tie, and the teams were declared co-champions because there was no overtime for championship games at that time. The Andalusia players didn't realize that, however. "Half of the team was getting ready for overtime before Coach [Don] Sharpe came over and told them, 'That's it, we're co-champs,'" Bill Anthony said.

The following season, Andalusia won the title outright, defeating Walter Wellborn of Anniston 7-0 in the championship game, solidifying the Bulldogs' status as a dynasty.

In 1978, Andalusia lost only one game, to Elba, ending its streak of 58 consecutive regular seasons without a loss, and it also kept the Bulldogs out of the playoffs.

Sharpe was the one mainly responsible for turning Andalusia into a state powerhouse in the 1970s. In 1958, Sharpe played on Andalusia's team that went 10-0 and won *The Birmingham News* Region 1 2A state championship.

During Sharpe's seven seasons as Andalusia's head coach, the Bulldogs went 58 consecutive regular-season games without a loss (57-0-1); won 50 consecutive regular-season games; recorded five undefeated regular seasons (1973, '74, '75, '76 and '77); played in state championship games four times in five years, claiming two states (one as co-champs) and finishing runners-up twice; and compiled a 64-4-1 regular-season record and 78-7-2 record overall.

"Coach Sharpe was the ultimate perfectionist who lived by the phrase 'perfect practice makes perfect' and not merely 'practice makes perfect,'" said Charles A. Short, a quarterback under Sharpe during that era.

"He instilled a winning attitude and work ethic," Bill Anthony said. "He was hard, but fair. He wanted us to do things the right way, and he was always pushing us to excel."

BLOUNT LEOPARDS (1990-98)

No one could have blamed Ben Harris if he had thrown up his hands and shouted, "What have I gotten myself into?" after taking over the Blount High football program in Prichard near Mobile. Harris accepted the job only three days before the start of practice for the 1988 season.

The previous season the team had won only one game, while losing nine.

On the first day of practice before the '88 season, only six players bothered to show up. Harris knew immediately he had to go on a recruiting mission, so he endeared himself to players and parents alike, preaching character and citizenship instead of football. He picked up players each Sunday to take them to church.

"One of the things I always have said is that I want to try to be a solution instead of the problem when it comes to young people," Harris said several years later. "It's tough coaching in the inner city with the drug problems, gangs, and violence. I started taking them to church, to college ball games and on different trips, so they could see the other side of the world."

Leopards' Championship Run		
Year	**Record**	**Finals result**
1990	13-2	W, Blount 36, Homewood 24
1991	13-2	L, Gadsden 20, Blount 7
1992	13-1	W, Blount 29, Russellville 15
1995	11-2	L, Homewood 17, Blount 12
1996	14-0	W, Blount 29, Saks 0
1997	12-3	W, Blount 21, Etowah 0
1998	14-0	W, Blount 27, Etowah 20 (OT)

Harris' methods worked. More players began coming out for football. His first team finished 6-6 and won the first playoff game in school history. Two years later in 1990, Blount won its first state title as former Alabama and Dallas Cowboys running back Sherman Williams became the first player in state history to rush for 3,000 yards in a season.

During the next eight years, the Leopards went on to win four more state championships, including three consecutively from 1996-98, and finish as runners-up twice, post two undefeated seasons and produce the first lineman to win the state's Mr. Football award, nose guard Demarco McNeil in 1998. Harris coached each one of those teams, except 1998 when Coach Cornelius Brown was at the helm.

HOOVER BUCCANEERS (2000-2005)

They call it "Hoover U." because of its spacious campus that houses a three-story 400,000-square-foot school building with tall concrete columns out front; an impressive athletic complex that's spread over 80 acres; and a student body that once approached 3,000 until a new high school (Spain Park) was built in the city near Birmingham.

To schools on the Hoover High Buccaneers' football schedule in the first six years of the 21st century, they must have seemed like a college team. Led by energetic head coach Rush Propst, who installed a spread offense that emphasizes the passing game when he arrived in 1999, Hoover completed the 2005 season by winning its unprecedented

Hoover players hoist the championship trophy after winning their second consecutive Class 6A title in 2003 at Legion Field. *Courtesy of Ed Tyler, prepsports.us*

fourth consecutive state championship in the largest classification in the state: Class 6A. Sidney Lanier won three Class 4A titles, when their were only four classes, in the first three years of the state playoff system in 1966-68. The title was also the Bucs' fifth in six years, and they were runners-up the year they didn't win it.

"It won't hit me until after I retire or leave here what we've accomplished," Propst said. "I don't know if I think of it as a dynasty. It could be close to being considered one, but we still have not won a national championship."

Throughout its run of success, Hoover has had to deal with accusations that it recruits players from other school districts and

Hoover players run onto the field before the 2005 Class 6A championship game, which they won for their fourth consecutive state title and fifth in six years.
Courtesy of Ed Tyler, prepsports.us

criticism that it wins because of its huge athletic budget for football and because its large student body gives it plenty of athletes to choose from.

"People say we've got numbers, but numbers have nothing to do with it," Propst bristled, while answering the critics. "People say that we've got all that money, but Hoover parents and players work hard to raise money for this program. People say we recruit players. That's illegal.

Bucs Dominance		
Year	Record	Finals result
2000	14-1	W, Hoover 28, Daphne 7
2001	14-1	L, Daphne 48, Hoover 21
2002	13-1	W, Hoover 39, Jeff Davis 29
2003	14-1	W, Hoover 22, Daphne 17
2004	15-0	W, Hoover 22, Prattville 7
2005	14-1	W, Hoover 56, Daphne 14

You don't have to recruit here. The place recruits itself. Winning championships recruits for Hoover."

Propst pointed out that Hoover hasn't had a considerable number of blue-chip prospects year in and year out. The Bucs' main two national recruits during their run of success were wide receiver Chad Jackson, who went to Florida, and quarterback John Parker Wilson, who wound up at Alabama.

"The main ingredient is hard work from the players to the assistant coaches, to the support staff, to me," Propst said.

HOMEWOOD PATRIOTS (2000-2005)

Please don't mention the "D" word in the company of Homewood head football coach Bob Newton when the subject of the Patriots' four state championships in six years from 2000-2005 comes up in conversation.

Although Newton's law of football means state titles—he also guided the Patriots to a state championship in 1995, his first season as head coach—he doesn't consider the Patriots' remarkable success to be a dynasty.

"Dynasty is a pretty strong word," Newton said. "I don't know if you can say it's a dynasty. I consider it a lot of good luck and good players. We've had some mighty good players."

Homewood's 21st century rise of power began with a thrilling five-overtime 41-34 victory against Benjamin Russell of Alexander City in the Class 5A championship game in 2000. Benjamin Russell avenged that loss in the finals in 2001, but Homewood bounced back from that loss by winning championships in 2002, 2004, and 2005. The Patriots reached the semifinals in 2003, but lost 34-7 to Briarwood Christian, a team they had beaten 24-14 during the regular season, to finish 12-2.

In 2005, the Patriots recorded the first unbeaten season (15-0) in school history, outscoring their opponents 429-79 during the regular season and 167-59 in the playoffs, including a 45-13 victory against Buckhorn in the championship game. They featured 33 seniors, including blue-chip college prospects Tim Hawthorne, a wide receiver

Homewood players celebrate after winning their second consecutive Class 5A championship in 2005 and fourth in six years. *Courtesy of Ed Tyler, prepsports.us*

who signed with Auburn, and David Ross, an offensive lineman who signed with Alabama. Quarterback Austin Hubbard also would have been in that category, but he elected to sign a baseball scholarship with Auburn. The star of the championship game, however, was senior

Patriots' Powerhouse		
Year	**Record**	**Finals result**
2000	13-2	W, Homewood 41, Benjamin Russell 34 (5 OT)
2001	14-1	L, Benjamin Russell 21, Homewood 13
2002	14-1	W, Homewood 31, Russellville 28
2004	14-1	W, Homewood 35, Russellville 21
2005	15-0	W, Homewood 45, Buckhorn 13

running back Steve Freeman, who rushed for 194 yards and four touchdowns on only nine carries.

Going unbeaten was something his players "really wanted," Newton said. "They played well and played with a purpose. Fifteen groups tried to stop them, but our bunch had a really good sense about what they wanted to accomplish. They worked hard all year long, and to see them do what they did was very gratifying."

VERBENA'S 50-GAME WIN STREAK (1950-55)

When James R. Porch left Oneonta in Blount County after the 1947 season and moved south to Verbena in Chilton County, some may have thought he had lost his mind.

His coaching career had begun at Oneonta in 1940 with a perfect 10-0 record. World War II and the U.S. Army beckoned, however, and he was fighting for his country over the next five years. When he returned to Oneonta in 1946, he promptly guided the team to a 9-1 record and then 9-0-1 in 1947—the only blemish a 19-19 tie to powerful Huntsville, one of the largest schools in the state.

When Porch arrived at Verbena in 1946, located in southern Chilton County just 40 miles from the state capital of Montgomery. The Red Devils had fallen on hard times. In fact, the 1947 season was a total disaster as Verbena went 0-10 and the Red Devils scored just 19 points all season—three touchdowns in 10 games. The program was in disarray, interest was at a low ebb, and the facilities were dismal.

The 1948 season produced immediate success as Porch led a group of fewer than 20 boys to a 7-3 record. He also headed a drive to light the modest football field by selling chances on a 1949 Ford, a single box of shotgun shells, and two pairs of nylon stockings. The poles were donated, and the Red Devils had lights that year.

Even with that success, no one was quite prepared for what would happen over the next seven years. Former player J. Harold Pierce described the evolution this way:

"When [Coach Porch] came to Verbena in 1948, he inherited what was left of a team that had lost all its games the year before and a program that was virtually nonexistent. We lost three games the first year, one the next, and then had five straight years when we went unbeaten. We had a streak of 50 straight unbeaten and untied games."

He said Porch mastered the turnaround with some basic tactics. "[Coach Porch] never taught anything but good, clean hard-hitting football."

His team in 1949 was 9-0 before Ramer downed Verbena 19-14 in the last game of the season. What happened next is what legends are made of and why there still stands in downtown Verbena a statue dedicated to Porch and his band of marauders who reeled off the 50 straight wins.

The streak began in 1950 with a 42-7 win over Jemison. Only a 2-0 win over Williams and a 14-7 triumph over Vincent gave fans much cause for concern as Verbena outscored 10 opponents 390-53.

"Coach Porch was all business. He never made the boys do side-straddle hops or pushups at practice," said former player Harold Patterson. "We lined up and did form blocking and tackling for 25 or 30 minutes [instead]. He always said, 'You don't side-straddle hop in a game. You block and tackle.' I never lost a game in my career. I never knew what it was like to lose a game."

Patterson also remembered a softer side of Porch and treasured how he provided the strong Christian example for his players. Patterson recalled one year how one player's parents were both sick. The kid had to stay home and pick cotton. Coach Porch went to the parents, promised that he and his wife and the rest of the team would come and pick the cotton on weekends if they would let their son continue to play," said Patterson. "And he delivered on his promise."

"Everyone in town always traveled to see us when we played. I mean everyone," Patterson continued. "Someone could have put Verbena in their pocket and walked away with it, because no one was left in town."

In 1951, Porch's team went 10-0 again, closing the season with a big 27-0 victory over county rival Clanton (Chilton County) as the Devils averaged 32.2 points per game and allowed just 6.5.

In 1952, a tougher schedule produced another 10-0 season—and 34.4 points per game. It also produced four shutouts and only one game

The Verbena Streak (1950-1955)

1950 (10-0)

Jemison	42-7
Isabella	43-7
Hicks Memorial	42-0
Goodwater	54-7
Billingsley	42-6
Williams	2-0
Vincent	14-7
Marbury	35-6
Elmore Co.	48-0
Ramar	68-13
Points	*390-53*

1951 (10-0)

Jemison	21-6
Loretto	33-0
Hicks Memorial	41-13
Goodwater	50-0
Billingsley	34-19
Vincent	20-0
Childersburg	19-0
Marbury	28-7
Elmore Co.	49-20
Chilton Co.	27-0
Points	*322-65*

1952 (10-0)

Jemison	28-0
Loretto	14-12
Hicks Memorial	33-0
Isabella	41-0
Calera	41-12
Vincent	40-6
Montevallo	40-18
Marbury	34-7
Billingsley	46-6
Chilton Co.	27-0
Points	*344-61*

1953 (9-0)

Jemison	41-0
Hicks Memorial	37-13
Isabella	41-6
Calera	27-6
Vincent	26-6
Montevallo	28-6
Marbury	7-0
Billingsley	33-6
Chilton Co.	12-7
Points	*252-50*

1954 (10-0)

Jemison	33-6
Elmore Co.	40-7
Isabella	42-0
Calera	41-0
Vincent	67-7
Montevallo	26-6
Marbury	48-0
Shelby Co.	27-0
Billingsley	47-12
Chilton Co.	14-6
Points	*385-44*

1955 (9-1)

Jemison	60-0
Elmore Co.	0-7 *streak ended*
Isabella	69-0
Calera	39-0
Vincent	62-7
Chilton Co.	7-6
Montevallo	41-6
Marbury	42-13
Shelby Co.	56-0
Billingsley	63-6
Points	*439-35*

that gave the swelling support cause for worry—a 14-12 win over Loretto in the second game of the season.

In 1953, a 9-0 record included a 7-0 win over Marbury and a 12-7 victory over Clanton. By then, the streak had reached 39 in a row and was getting national attention.

In 1954, a 33-6 win over Jemison jump-started another 10-0 season as the Red Devils averaged 38.5 points per game and allowed only 4.4. Only one team scored more than seven points—Billingsley in week nine's 47-12 rout. Again, Chilton County provided the most drama as Verbena registered its 49th win in a row in the last game of the season with a 14-6 win.

The entire state turned its eyes to Verbena when the 1955 season opened. Already owning three *Birmingham News* small-school state championship trophies for the 1951, 1953 and 1954 seasons, the Red Devils opened with a 60-0 shellacking of Jemison for the 50th win. The next week, however, Elmore County of Eclectic shut out the Red Devils 7-0 and snapped the longest unbeaten and untied streak in state history at the time. It was finally broken by Clay County (1994-1997) when the Panthers reeled off 55 wins in a row.

Following that setback, Porch regrouped his lads for a 69-0 pounding of Isabella and coasted home with seven straight wins to go 9-1. And again, *The Birmingham News* named tiny Verbena as the state's best small-school program in the state as Verbena outscored 10 opponents 439-35 while registering four shutouts.

In 1956, Porch guided the Red Devils to a 7-2-1 record—closing an incredible run that produced an 81-7-1 slate in 10 seasons. He left for one year at Fort Payne (6-4) in 1957 before retiring as a head coach.

Porch's career totals were 115-12-2. He went into the AHSAA Sports Hall of Fame in 1992, and little Verbena High School went into the state's records books as a legend for all time. Former players have a reunion every June—meeting at the monument to celebrate that glorious time in Alabama prep football history.

CLAY COUNTY'S STREAK

Alabama's longest prep winning streak of all time had quite an inconspicuous beginning in 1994. Clay County's Panthers, a tiny Class 2A team located almost dead-center in Alabama at Ashland, had not won a state championship since the state playoffs were commenced in 1967. So when Class 4A powerhouse Cleburne County nipped young coach Danny Horn's team 3-0 to start the 1994 season, the rest of the state had no way of knowing what really was in store.

But Horn, with a veteran defensive coordinater in the school's head basketball coach Jerry Weems, had some inkling. Weems had directed the Panthers to back-to-back state basketball titles in 1991 and 1992 while Horn was quietly molding what would turn out to be the greatest small-school defense in state history.

"We felt like shutting down Cleburne County without a touchdown was a good sign," said Horn. "We had a bunch of really hungry and

Clay County coach Danny Horn hugs quarterback Chase Horn, his son, after the Panthers won the 2005 Class 2A championship. *Courtesy of Ed Tyler, prepsports.us*

quick kids on defense. They really knew how to get after you. And Coach Weems was not just a great basketball coach. He knew his football, too."

Cleburne County would go on to win 14 straight games before losing to T.R. Miller in the Class 4A state finals that season. Clay County would win the final 14 of the 1994 campaign—including a 24-0 victory on the road at Gordo in the 2A finals.

By the time the Panthers would lose again, Clay County would own a state-record 55 straight wins, including 34 by shutouts, and three consecutive state championships.

The defensive domination in 1994 has never been equaled. In 15 games, the Panthers defense allowed only two touchdowns all season and 22 total points in 15 games. Opponents had less than 100 yards total offense per game.

The 1995 season was more of the same as Clay County opened with a 25-0 shutout of Cleburne County and then reeled off three more shutouts before Vincent scored the first TD of the season against the defense anchored by All-State linemen Vernon Marable, RaJohn Myles, and future Auburn University safety Stanford Simmons.

Even that TD was hard to come by. Vincent blocked a punt, the only blocked punt in the 55-game streak, and recovered the ball inside the 5-yard line. Four plays netted only a couple of yards, and Clay County took over—fumbling on first down. It took four more plays before the Yellow Jackets could crack the goal line.

Clay County would then reel off five more shutouts—giving Horn's team nine total—and won perhaps the most thrilling state championship game in Class 2A state history at home in a downpour in December of 1995 with a 7-6 win over the state's winningest playoff team of all time, Hazlewood.

Fans gathered at Ashland's small stadium as early as noon on the championship game day and many sat in the pouring rain all afternoon to secure their seats.

It took a little trickery to secure the win, however. After receiving the second-half kickoff, Clay County switched to an unbalanced line—something the visitors from Town Creek had not seen on film, and with

Clay County's Streak

1994 (14-1)	Score	Class	Streak	1996 (15-0)	Score	Class	Streak
Cleburne Co.	0-3	4A	L	Cleburne Co.	45-0	4A	W-30
Elmore Co.	9-0	3A	W-1	Elmore Co.	54-0	4A	W-31
Central-Coosa	39-0	4A	W-2	Central-Coosa	45-0	4A	W-32
Randolph Co.	33-0	4A	W-3	Daleville	30-0	4A	W-33
Vincent	22-6	2A	W-4	Randolph Co.	42-0	2A	W-34
Bibb Graves	40-0	1A	W-5	Winterboro	50-0	2A	W-35
Winterboro	62-0	2A	W-6	Reeltown	47-0	2A	W-36
Talladega Central	25-0	2A	W-7	Beulah	79-12	2A	W-37
Horseshoe Bend	47-0	2A	W-8	Horseshoe Bend	14-6	2A	W-38
Lineville	29-3	2A	W-9	Lineville	21-0	2A	W-39
Playoffs				Playoffs			
Excel	48-0	2A	W-10	Straughn	47-0	2A	W-40
Brantley	6-3	2A	W-11	Paramount	35-0	2A	W-41
Georgiana	7-0	2A	W-12	Cottonwood	27-10	2A	W-42
Leroy	17-6	2A	W-13	Luverne	37-14	2A	W-43
Gordo	24-0*	2A	W-14	Lineville	42-0*	2A	W-44
*-State 2A finals				*-State 2A finals			
1994 Season totals:				*1996 Season totals:*			
Points:	*408*			*Points:*	*615*		
Points allows:	*22*			*Points allows:*	*42*		
Shutouts:	*(10)*			*Shutouts:*	*(11)*		
1995 (15-0)	Score	Class	Streak	1997 (11-1)	Score	Class	Streak
Cleburne Co.	25-0	4A	W-15	Cleburne Co.	14-7	4A	W-45
Elmore Co.	56-0	3A	W-16	Elmore Co.	21-0	4A	W-46
Central-Coosa	40-0	4A	W-17	Central-Coosa	48-8	4A	W-47
Randolph Co.	54-0	4A	W-18	Daleville	16-13	4A	W-48
Vincent	44-6	2A	W-19	Randolph Co.	48-0	2A	W-49
Bibb Graves	70-7	1A	W-20	Winterboro	50-8	2A	W-50
Winterboro	48-3	2A	W-21	Reeltown	43-16	2A	W-51
Talladega Central	62-0	2A	W-22	Beulah	35-0	2A	W-52
Horseshoe Bend	41-0	2A	W-23	Horseshoe Bend	33-8	2A	W-53
Lineville	26-6	2A	W-24	Lineville	10-7	2A	W-54
Playoffs				Playoffs			
Highland Home	35-0	2A	W-25	Paramount	40-0	2A	W-55
Reeltown	44-14	2A	W-26	Luverne	14-21 (OT)	2A	L
Lineville	28-0	2A	W-27	1997 Season totals:			
Georgiana	49-0	2A	W-28	*Points:*	*350*		
Hazlewood	7-6*	2A	W-29	*Points allows:*	*88*		
*-State 2A finals				*Shutouts:*	*(4)*		
1995 Season totals:							
Points:	*601*						
Points allows:	*42*						
Shutouts:	*(9)*						

the heavy rain as a shield, the Panthers drove to the game's only touchdown—kicking the all-important extra point.

Hazlewood almost won on the ensuing kickoff, but a shoestring tackle inside the Clay 20-yard line left the Bears short of the end zone.

In 1996, with the AHSAA moving all the state championships from home fields to Birmingham's 80,000-seat Legion Field, Clay County took up right where it left off—and then some.

After seven straight shutout wins, Clay County had outscored its opponents 313-0. In week eight, Beulah threw two TD passes against defensive back coach Kris Herron's secondary in a 79-12 rout. The Bobcats scores came with junior high kids in the lineup late. Still, Herron caught quite a lot of ribbing from his fellow coaches.

By the time Clay County beat archrival Lineville 21-0 in week 10 and again 42-0 at Legion Field in the 2A championship game, his secondary was yielding only 42 yards through the air per game.

With a lot of new faces in the lineup in 1997, Clay County still went unbeaten through 10 regular-season games and the first round of the state playoffs to run the streak to 55. Ironically, it was another rain storm that led to the streak's demise. Playing at Luverne in round two of the state playoffs, it rained most of the day and left the field soaked. Coach Butch Norman's Tigers forced a fumble to beat the Panthers 21-14.

Norman, a former University of Alabama and Canadian Football League lineman, turned to his own high school coach, legendary Glenn Daniel, to set up the game plan that finally ended the streak. Daniel, the state's coach with the most career wins (302) before retiring in the early 1990s, came out of retirement to serve on his favorite pupil's staff.

The Streak (Year by Year)						
Year	Record	Pts	Opp	Avg.	Opp avg.	Shutouts
1994	14-1	408	22	27.2	1.5	10
1995	15-0	601	42	40.1	2.8	9
1996	15-0	615	42	41.0	2.8	11
1997	11-1	350	88	29.5	7.3	4
TOT	55-2	1,974	194	34.6	3.4	34

Luverne went on to destroy Sand Rock in the state finals 51-14 at Legion Field three weeks later.

When the Clay County streak was finally over, the Panthers had rolled up 1,960 points in 55 wins and allowed just 170 points in the same stretch. The streak also included 16 straight playoff wins.

Clay County also claimed state titles in 2000, 2002 (1A), and again in 2005 and headed into the 2006 season with a brand-new 15-game win streak intact.

CHAMPIONSHIP ALLEY

Travel west along Highway 72 in northwest Alabama, and you will come across the small cities of Courtland, Town Creek, and Leighton. As far as high school football is concerned, the 20-mile stretch of road through those communities could be called "Championship Alley."

Since the AHSAA instituted a playoff system in 1966, the Courtland (now R.A. Hubbard) Chiefs, Hazlewood Golden Bears in Town Creek, and the Colbert County Indians have appeared in a combined 34 championship games and won 22 titles, including Colbert County's co-championship in 1979.

Hazlewood has been the most successful of the trio, winning a state-record 11 championships in 14 final appearances. The Golden Bears also hold the record for most consecutive titles with five from 1988-1992.

The Golden Bears won their first title in 1970. Johnny Yates was a backup quarterback on that team and later was the school's principal during Hazlewood's streak of five consecutive championships.

"We were undefeated, 13-0," Yates said of the '70 championship. "The community was fired up and the tradition and pride snowballed in the '70s."

Hazlewood had another great team in 1971, going 9-1, but it did not advance to the playoffs. "That was the time of integration," Yates said. "They closed the black school, Central, and integrated Courtland High School and Hazlewood. There was a mix-up in the transcripts of one of the black players, and we had to forfeit two or three games."

"The [winning] tradition may have started at Central. They had great athletes."

Clyde Goode Sr. played at Central and is the father of Chris, Kerry, Pierre, and Clyde Jr., and the uncle of Antonio Langham. They all played starring roles on several of Hazlewood's championship teams.

Courtland didn't become a powerhouse in the AHSAA until the 1980s, but during segregation in the late 1950s and throughout the 1960s, Central Courtland Colored High School was a dynasty under Coach Hoover White.

White took over at his alma mater as head football coach and track coach in 1956. During the next 14 years, his football teams had a record of 86-22-3, won seven conference championships, and put together a 28-game winning streak. He was conference Coach of the Year in 1960, and his track teams won six conference championships.

After Central Courtland Colored High School and Courtland High School were consolidated, White served as principal of the combined school from 1972-76.

Hazlewood in the Finals		
Year	Class	Result
1970	1A	W, Hazlewood 44, Ohatchee 0
1975	2A	W, Hazlewood 53, Hokes Bluff 0
1978	2A	L, Elmore County 7, Hazlewood 6
1981	1A	W, Hazlewood 28, McKenzie 0
1982	2A	W, Hazlewood 24, Dadeville 16
1985	2A	W, Hazlewood 23, Autaugaville 16
1988	2A	W, Hazlewood 28, New Brockton 0
1989	2A	W, Hazlewood 75, Georgiana 0
1990	2A	W, Hazlewood 14, Cottonwood 0
1991	2A	W, Hazlewood 32, Reeltown 22
1992	2A	W, Hazlewood 37, Reeltown 6
1993	2A	L, St. Clair County 18, Hazlewood 13
1995	2A	L, Clay County 7, Hazlewood 6
2000	1A	W, Hazlewood 23, Reeltown 16

Total appearances: 14; record 11-3

Hoover White's brother, Louis White, took over the Courtland program in the late 1970s and guided the Chiefs for 24 years, compiling a 186-80 record, making 17 playoff appearances and winning four state championships, including three in a row from 1988-1990. The other came in 1995.

Courtland also won a state championship in 1999 with a former Hazlewood player, Lymos McDonald, as the Chiefs' head coach.

Colbert County traces its run of championships to C.T. Manley, who once described himself as "a full-time coach, teacher, and janitor." Manley took over as the Indians' coach in 1954 and remained there until 1979 when he went to Muscle Shoals. He explained his coaching philosophy thusly: "I teach boys that want to learn and want to win. We don't have any forced summer program, as most of our boys come from the country. They eat what they want to, they don't have to lift weights all the time, and they play football because they love it."

Manley fashioned a 171-78-7 record at Colbert County and led his 1972 team to a 13-0 record and the Class 3A state championship, featuring quarterback Phil Gargis and receivers Ozzie Newsome and Thad Flanagan. Gargis wound up at Auburn and Flanagan and Newsome at Alabama. Newsome, the current general manager of the NFL's Baltimore Ravens, is in the Pro Football Hall of Fame.

The Indians continued their success under Coach Don Creasy, who coached his alma mater to 11 playoff appearances in 12 seasons and a

Courtland/R.A. Hubbard in the Finals		
Year	**Class**	**Result**
1986	1A	L, Sweet Water 26, Courtland 14
1988	1A	W, Courtland 22, Billingsley 21
1989	1A	W, Courtland 13, Excel 2
1990	1A	W, Courtland 18, Autaugaville 0
1991	1A	L, McKenzie 15, Courtland 7
1995	1A	W, Courtland 14, Maplesville 7
1999	1A	W, Courtland 13, Brantley 10
2004	1A	L, Sweet Water 35, R.A. Hubbard 7
Total appearances: 8; record 5-3		

Colbert County in the Finals		
Year	**Class**	**Result**
1967	3A	L, Russellville 13, Colbert County 6
1972	3A	W, Colbert County 41, Cullman 14
1978	3A	L, Eufaula 29, Colbert County 0
1979	3A	T, Colbert County 0, Jackson 0 (co-champs)
1985	5A	W, Colbert County 26, Dora 13
1989	4A	L, Pike County 20, Colbert County 19
1993	3A	W, Colbert County 14, St. Paul's 10
1994	3A	W, Colbert County 17, Luverne 10
1996	3A	W, Colbert County 25, UMS-Wright 19 (2 OT)
1997	3A	L, Aliceville 21, Colbert County 19 (OT)
2000	3A	L, Aliceville 50, Colbert County 7
2002	3A	L, T.R. Miller 38, Colbert County 6
Total appearances: 12; record 5-6-1		

record of 101-16, while winning two state championships (1979 and 1985) and finishing as runner-up twice.

In the 1990s, Coach Jimmie Moore guided Colbert County to three more state titles ('93, '94, and '96). The 1996 title, a 25-19 double-overtime victory against UMS-Wright of Mobile in the first year of the Super Six Championships at Legion Field, came while Moore was battling cancer, which claimed his life a few years later.

T.R. MILLER: CONSISTENT EXCELLENCE

When it comes to high school football dynasties in Alabama, no program has been more consistent through time than T.R. Miller of Brewton.

A powerhouse in the 1940s and early 1950s, the Tigers fell on some hard times in the late 1950s that continued into the early 1960s. However, things began to change later in the decade when brothers Bucky and Mack Phillippi arrived on the scene. When the state playoff system was instituted by the Alabama High School Athletic Association in 1966, the excitement in this south Alabama town in Escambia

County just north of the Florida border was united with one cause—
T.R. Miller football.

The state playoffs for all schools began in Alabama in 1967, and by
1969, the Tigers, coached then by Mack Wood, won their first state
title. Quarterback Bucky Phillippi directed T.R. Miller to a 41-14 win
over Abbeville in the semifinals and a 27-0 over Aliceville in the Class
2A finals.

By the time the Tigers won the 3A state crown at Birmingham's
Legion Field over Colbert County 38-7 in 2002, T.R. Miller had
captured six championships and had finished as runner-up another six
times. In 2003, 2004, and 2005, the Tigers lost in the semifinals.

The amazing domination reached a new high when the AHSAA went
to six classifications in 1984. The Tigers won the 4A crown over
Cherokee County that season, then won in 1991, 1994, and 2000 and
won more games than any other team in the state in the 1990s.

"There's no one thing you can put your finger on," said coach Jamie
Riggs, only the fourth head coach at the school since Wood won the
first state crown almost 40 years prior. Riggs became the youngest coach
in AHSAA history to win 200 games in 2005.

"I grew up here in the 1960s, and I remember going to the games and
watching the Phillippi boys play," Riggs said. "Football games were a
social event then. They still are."

T.R. Miller averaged almost 12 wins a season through the 1990s and
the first six seasons of the 2000 decade—all under Riggs' watch.

"There is so much community support," he said. "We have had a
great administration. We go back three and four generations with some
of our players. It means an awful lot to play football at T.R. Miller and
wear this red and black jersey. And I think another big reason for our
success has been a supportive administration and a group of assistant
coaches I think are the best anywhere."

The school got its name from a local lumber magnate, T.R. Miller,
who provided most of the jobs for this blue-collar town. County rival
W.S. Neal High School was built by one of Miller's friends and business
associates, said Riggs.

The two schools square off annually in a game billed simply as "The Battle of Murder Creek." The creek got its name from a fatal robbery along its banks in 1788. One of those arrested was later hanged on the exact spot.

The creek divides Brewton and East Brewton—in essence, T.R. Miller and W.S. High Schools.

While Miller has dominated the series through the years, W.S. Neal had its moments. When Calvin Culliver was in the backfield, the Blue Eagles were one of the top programs anywhere—reaching the 1971 Class 3A finals before falling to Tarrant at Birmingham's Legion Field 34-20. Culliver went on to have an outstanding career at the University of Alabama.

Riggs said the tradition at T.R. Miller is based more on the "average kids." "Through the years, we have had our share of stars, but most years it is those other kids who keep the tradition going."

Among the "stars" has been former Alabama quarterback Walter Lewis, who won the national punt, pass, and kick title as a youngster. He quarterbacked Coach Paul "Bear" Bryant's last team in 1982 and finished ninth in the voting for the Heisman Trophy.

In all, four former T.R. Miller Tigers have reached the NFL or CFL.

ALABAMA SCHOOL FOR DEAF IS BEST IN THE LAND

Each player in the football lineup was deaf. The head coach on the sidelines was also deaf. And most of the overflow crowd that packed Alabama School for the Deaf's small stadium in Talladega that cold night in October, 2000, was also deaf.

Why then, was there so much noise?

It could have been the drum on the sidelines. The drum, equipped with a student drummer, was used to signal the cadence for the team on the field. One blast meant snap the ball on the first count. Two blasts meant on the second count. And three blasts—well—that normally meant the other team had just jumped off sides.

ASD coach Walter Ripley addresses his 2000 team. *Courtesy of Alabama School for the Deaf*

On this particular night, the Silent Warriors were facing the nation's top-ranked football-playing deaf school, Eastern North Carolina School for the Deaf. ASD had won 28 straight games versus other deaf schools and could set a new national record with the win. Also unbeaten against other deaf schools that season, a win coupled with a season-ending victory over Model School for the Deaf in Washington D.C. the next week would likely mean the school's fourth national championship in school history. ASD won previous national titles in 1971, 1987, and 1991. The Warriors also had six national boys deaf school national basketball titles to its credit.

They reached both goals, breaking the win-streak mark with an 18-12 victory over Eastern North Carolina in a dramatic come-from-behind win. By season's end, head football coach Walter Ripley's ASD Silent Warriors had extended the win streak to 31. And when it finally ended two years later, the win streak had reached 38 games. Ripley, like his players, was also deaf.

ASD, 6-4 overall, went 4-0 against other deaf schools, beating Tennessee 48-8, Florida 16-8, Eastern North Carolina 18-12, and Model Secondary School of Washington D.C., 34-13. The final game was played on the campus of Gallaudet University, a college founded for deaf students, in Washington, D.C.

Both goals were never more threatened than the night they played Eastern North Carolina School. "This was the toughest win out of all 29 victories," said Ripley. "This is craziest game I've coached in. We never would have imagined we would have won the game in the last four minutes. It was nearly impossible."

ASD, which opened its doors as a special school for the state's deaf and blind students in 1958, first started playing football continuously in 1892—going against mostly college varsity and junior varsity teams.

Late in the fourth quarter of this game—played 108 years later—the Silent Warriors were trailing 12-0 with just over four minutes remaining when defensive end Brian Moss crashed through the Eastern North Carolina wall of blockers to tackle punter Robert Webber in the end zone for a safety.

Following the free kick, ASD rode the arm of quarterback Courtney Walker to a touchdown with 2:41 remaining. Johnson connected with Corey Johnson for a 35-yard TD. Mike Maxwell scored the two-point conversion to close the score to 12-10.

Still, the Silent Warriors were going to have to give up the football to the visitors. The defense, which held Eastern North Carolina's star runner Jon Lambeth to just 90 yards rushing on 28 carries, forced another punt with just over a minute to play. Maxwell returned the kick 20 yards to set up the game-winning touchdown three plays later.

Maxwell, who had 113 return yards on the night, was the target of Walker's next pass completion. He caught the ball, then fought through the defense to complete the 30-yard scoring play with 54.9 seconds remaining to set off an emotional celebration for the ASD fans. Mike Baker, a 6-foot-6, 250-pound senior tight end, caught the two-point conversion pass from Walker to close out the scoring. "This is the best day in my life from the time I first picked up a football," Maxwell told the media on hand.

Don Hackney, who was inducted into the Alabama High School Sports Hall of Fame in 2006, served as athletic director and head basketball coach for more than three decades at ASD. He also served on the football staff most of those years. He is not deaf.

It was under his direction that ASD became the most dominant deaf school athletic program in the nation in the 1990s. He brought Ripley on board.

Hackney guided the Silent Warriors to six national boys basketball championships and won 485 games as ASD earned the moniker "Home of Champions." A tragic accident a few years ago—he fell from a ladder while repairing his roof—left him paralyzed from the chest down. The fall didn't deter his spirit, however, as students and alumni nationwide rushed to his aid financially and emotionally and through prayer.

"Stability among the coaches is the main reason for success of ASD in football [and basketball]," said Barry Strassler, editor of a national newspaper and newsletter for the deaf, who had praise for Hackney and Ripley. "Walter Ripley is a rarity among deaf school coaches. He has been at the helm for a decade in a profession where turnover is high. Other schools should try to emulate the ASD formula for success."

6

GREAT RIVALS

THE CLAY BOWL:
CLAY COUNTY VS. LINEVILLE

labama's prep football history is dotted with tremendous rivalries in every corner of the state. None is more fierce than the Clay Bowl—played between two schools located in the very center of the state.

Clay County and Lineville have been squaring off in the Clay Bowl since 1922. And while the rivalry was fierce from the beginning, it reached a new intensity in the 1990s when Lineville's Aggies and Clay County's Panthers battled for the state championship.

Clay County, a farming and timber tract of Alabama's landscape, has had some famous alumni—such as Alabama's current governor Bob Riley and Super Bowl participant and All-Pro NFL lineman Howard Ballard.

The two main cities, Ashland and Lineville, are separated by a creek and a bridge with downtown to downtown not more than five miles apart. To call these two normally tranquil communities "cities" is somewhat of a misnomer. They are actually quiet villages of hard-working patriots 51 weeks of the year.

It is that 52nd week that has grabbed the attention of the nation. The rivalry was judged one of the nation's 10 best high school rivalries by *USA Today* and *Sports Illustrated*—and for good reason.

While Lineville held a 51-39-4 edge after the 2005 season—which included a 19-0 loss in the regular season and a 16-12 loss in the Class 2A playoff semifinals—Clay County has actually dominated the series in the last decade.

The Panthers actually have dominated just about everyone else in that time span, too—reeling off a state-record 55 consecutive wins from 1994-1997.

Clay won the first game of the series in 1922 handily (39-0). Lineville won the 1961 game 48-0. On 10 different occasions, the two teams have met twice in the same year, including 1922, 1942, 1943, 1944, 1945, 1946, 1995, 1996, 1998, and 2005.

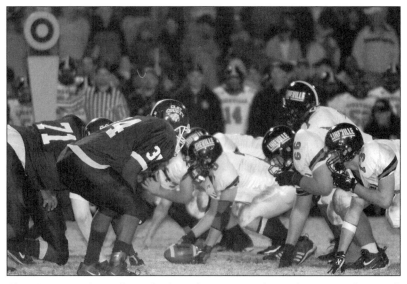

Clay County and Lineville at the line of scrimmage during the 2005 Clay Bowl.
Courtesy of Ed Tyler, prepsports.us

Ironically, in 1996, the AHSAA placed Ashland in Region 5 and Lineville in Region 4—setting up the first and only time the two teams have met in the state finals.

The Panthers won the regular-season meeting 21-0. Both teams advanced through the state playoffs and reached the 2A championship game at Legion Field in '96, but the Aggies hobbled in with several key injuries. Clay County's defense that season, arguably the best small-school defense in state history, made things worse for the Aggies real quick when Lineville's quarterback was knocked out of the game. By the time the final horn had sounded, Clay County had won its third straight Class 2A state championship 42-0.

Lineville has reached the Super 6 finals four times since the championships were moved to Legion Field in 1996 but has yet to win a title. Clay County has been to the finals in either 2A or 1A four times as well—winning each time: 1996, 2000, 2002, and 2005.

Each team has won seven straight in the series. Lineville has posted 21 shutouts and Clay County 23. The four ties came in 1924, 1942, 1946, and 1953. Three were scoreless ties and one, 1953, was 13-13.

The Clay Bowl has been decided by one point four times and by a touchdown or less 23 times. The largest known crowd at the game was at the 1998 semifinals at Lineville—estimated at close to 7,000 in a 3,000-seat stadium.

"This is the biggest event of the year," said Clay County coach Danny Horn, who guided the Panthers through each of the 55 wins in the fabled streak. "A lot of our kids go to the same churches. The two towns are close, and we get along most of the time. "The bragging rights are important for the winner."

Fans come early the week of the Clay Bowl, tying down cushions and chairs as early as Monday. The game actually provided a first of sorts for big business when some Lineville fans pooled their money together and rented the home economics room located in the Ashland school at the north end of the stadium to watch the game. With more than 2,000 fans standing around the fence, seats were pretty much useless as the fans' view was impeded.

But in the "skybox," elevated some six feet above the playing surface, Lineville fans gathered and enjoyed the delights of fried chicken, mashed potatoes, and iced tea as they watched from the window.

The fee was reportedly a whopping $100—donated to the home economics department at Clay County High School.

HAZLEWOOD VS. COURTLAND (NOW R.A. HUBBARD)

The two small schools in Lawrence County in northwest Alabama are just five miles apart in Town Creek and Courtland. Neither city has more than 1,500 residents, but that doesn't stop the schools from being football powerhouses.

Throughout the 1980s and 1990s they boasted two of the top programs in the state. From 1988-1995, the Hazlewood Golden Bears and Courtland Chiefs combined to win nine state titles (Hazlewood five and Courtland four.) They reached the finals in either 1A or 2A another three times.

The two schools began playing each other twice a year in the late 1980s when both teams found difficulty scheduling games. "It would be hard to beat this rivalry," former Hazlewood coach Ricky Johnson said. "A lot of these people work together. When we played, half of the people in the stadium are standing. We drew an estimated 4,000 to 5,000 people in a small stadium, and people put on a fashion show."

Hazlewood had to endure one of the more embarrassing moments in the rivalry in the early 1990s. "Alabama had just won the (college football) national championship and they had an All-American from our school [defensive back Antonio Langham], and they signed three players from our team," Johnson recalled. "ESPN asked them to give it a name of a school that was a football hotbed, and they told them about us.

"Three weeks before the season opened, ESPN came to our practice, and they came by on the day of the game when we played at Courtland. ESPN taped our practice and some of the Courtland folks started saying ESPN went to Town Creek because Courtland wasn't good enough.

"When we ran out for pregame warmups, ESPN's big, bright lights were on us, and everybody was watching Hazlewood. Even the Courtland fans were watching us.

"Courtland had just had some players quit before the season started, but they kicked our tails. They blocked two punts and beat us 13-0. It was very embarrassing, and afterward there was a lot of talk going on. That was hard to swallow."

THE BATTLE OF MURDER CREEK: T.R. MILLER VS. W.S. NEAL

The rivalry between the T.R. Miller Tigers and W.S. Neal Eagles goes back more than 60 years and is one of the few neighboring rivalries that has a colorful name—aptly called the "Battle of Murder Creek."

The two schools are located in Brewton and East Brewton in Escambia County, with Murder Creek dividing the two communities. The creek is called that because of a fatal robbery along its banks in 1788 and the subsequent hanging of one of the assailants in the same spot.

In the 1920s, Brewton had more millionaires per capita than any other city in the U.S. East Brewton was the blue-collar side of town. The two sides are friendly until the battle begins. "It's something the communities look forward to," T.R. Miller coach Jamie Riggs said. "What makes it so unique is so many parents went to Miller or Neal and intermarried. It's always been a big game. It's not just the schools playing, it's the two schools playing."

And when the teams take the field against each other, the stadium is packed. "The communities together have only 6,000 or 7,000 people, and generally we draw 5,000 or 6,000 when we play," Riggs said. "It's a tremendous atmosphere, especially when we play at Neal. Neal has a smaller stadium, and the stands are closer to the field. The stands are full at 5 p.m., and folks are standing everywhere.

"It's great for players to be part of that once in a lifetime. It makes them feel special."

Blaine Hathcock got his first taste of the Miller-Neal rivalry in 2005 after taking over as the Eagles' head coach. He had been an assistant at Pell City, Hamilton, and Handley. "I've never been around anything like this rivalry," Hathcock told the *Mobile Register*. "Every person I met when I got here introduced themselves and then they tell you, 'I'm a Miller person,' or 'I'm a Neal person.' That's the way you introduce yourself. It's all-consuming for the whole community."

Miller has held a decided upper hand over the last 20 years. Neal has beaten Miller just once since 1986.

ROBERT E. LEE-MONTGOMERY VS. SIDNEY LANIER

For years, Sidney Lanier was the only public school for white students in segregated Montgomery. George Washington Carver and Booker T. Washington were the two black schools.

As Montgomery's population began to increase, another school for whites had to be built, and up sprang Robert E. Lee High in 1955. Its arrival also gave birth to one of the state's great high school football rivalries.

"They were the two biggest schools in the state," said Spence McCracken, who played at Lee and also coached the Generals for 11 years before becoming head coach at Opelika High School. "All the white folks in Montgomery went to one school or the other, and they played football against each other, it was the only show in town. It was incredible because 25,000 people came out every time they played. You had to stand in long lines to get tickets."

The most dramatic game of the rivalry occurred in 1966 when the Generals and Poets played for the first state championship of the newly adopted Alabama High School Athletic Association playoffs. The playoffs were installed for 4A schools in 1966 with four teams advancing to the postseason. The playoffs were added for Classes 3A, 2A, and 1A the next season.

Lanier had beaten Lee 10-0 in the final game of the 1966 regular season, but both advanced to the four-team state playoffs. In the semifinals, Lanier routed and Lee crushed to set up a rematch. The rematch was televised—the first high school football game to be televised—in Montgomery. Lanier prevailed again, 9-7, to claim the state title before more than 25,000 spectators. The game ended with Lee trying a long field goal twice. Lanier jumped off sides the first time as time expired, but since the game couldn't end on the penalty, the Generals got another chance to kick but failed.

"I'd have to say one of the reasons the 1966 game had so much interest was because it was the first," said McCracken, a starting center and linebacker for Lee at the time. "It was the only game being played, and it also pitted what was then the state's two biggest schools, both from the same town. Lee and Lanier were the best two teams in Alabama that year. I don't think anyone will argue that point. In Montgomery, it was bigger than the Auburn-Alabama game."

The Poets won the next two Class 4A titles as well before the Generals ascended to the throne in 1969 and 1970.

"Every time they played, it was a party atmosphere," Wiley Cutts, a teacher at Lanier in 1966 who became principal of the school in 1972, said in a *Montgomery Advertiser* story about the 1966 game. "There wasn't any studying going on. We were at the mercy of the rivalry. Those were exciting games. For a week, that's all it was. We had pep rallies every day—spontaneous. It was unlike anything I had ever experienced."

Integration and the arrival of Jeff Davis High School in 1970 diminished the Lee-Lanier rivalry.

"It was a good rivalry, but Jeff Davis and Lee got bigger than Lee and Lanier," McCracken said.

BANKS VS. WOODLAWN

When Banks High School opened on the east side of Birmingham in 1957, the majority of its students came from nearby Woodlawn High.

Woodlawn was a football powerhouse among the Big 5 schools in the city, and it had so many boys come out for football that it didn't have enough uniforms to go around. For those players, the opening of Banks was a godsend.

It also laid the groundwork for one of the fiercest football rivalries in the state throughout the 1960s and early 1970s. "The rivalry started with the kids coming from the same neighborhoods," said George "Shorty" White, who was the head football coach at Banks from 1960 through 1974. "Banks opened with a ninth grade in 1957, mainly drawing kids from Woodlawn. We had one side of First Avenue, and they had the other side.

"We became rivals in every sport, including track, basketball, and baseball. It was like a brother vs. brother thing."

The football rivalry, however, was the most intense. Banks played primarily a junior varsity schedule in its first two years of existence to become established. The Jets finally met the Colonels in 1960. "The kids who had transferred from Woodlawn as freshmen were seniors, and we beat them," White said. "Then we went to the Crippled Children's Classic and beat Ensley."

Banks had its share of star players, including Johnny Musso and the Rutledge boys, Gary and Jeff. Woodlawn had its standouts, too, including running back Tony Nathan.

The most memorable game of the rivalry occurred in 1974 when Nathan and Jeff Rutledge were seniors and both teams were 9-0 with a playoff berth on the line. The largest crowd—42,000-plus—turned out to watch Banks defeat Woodlawn 18-7.

After Huffman High opened in the early 1970s, the Banks-Woodlawn rivalry diminished because Huffman became Banks' chief rival. Eventually, with enrollment declining, Banks became a middle school.

VIGOR VS. BLOUNT

Until 2005, the Vigor Wolves and Blount Leopards were located one mile apart in Prichard, near Mobile. Blount moved into a new building on the western edge of town and after years of sharing Prichard Stadium, the teams played at the Leopards' on-campus stadium. But that didn't diminish their rivalry.

"Most of the kids grow up together," said former Vigor head coach James Perine. "They start school together in elementary and junior high, then when they get to high school, they split up. Sometimes it's cousins against cousins and brothers against brothers. "They have community involvement together, church involvement, and recreational involvement."

At Philadelphia Baptist Church in Prichard, the congregation separates during service the Sunday before the big game. "They divide it up," Blount coach Ben Harris said. "All Blount fans on one side. All Vigor fans on the other side."

Vigor's winning ways go way, way back—all the way to the days of Scott Hunter in the mid-1960s and before. And in the 1980s, the Wolves were the toast of Class 6A with back-to-back state titles under the direction of Harold Clark in 1987 and 1988. Darrell "Lectron" Williams, Cleon Jones, Jr., Mitch Davis, and current NFL lineman Willie Anderson are just a few of the more than 100 players who went on to college stardom in an incredible 15-year stretch. Blount lost more games in the 1980s than any 5A team in the state—and all its games to cross-town rival Vigor.

The rivalry took a mighty turn in the 1990s, however. Ben Harris arrived as Blount's coach and immediately took the Leopards from the bottom to the top—thanks in part to players such as Sherman Williams, Dameyune Craig, DeMarco McNeil, and DeAndre Green. Blount won state titles in 1990, 1992, 1996, 1997, and 1998, and finished second in 1991 and 1995.

The rivalry reached its zenith in 1998 when more than 19,000 fans crammed into 10,000-seat Prichard Stadium to watch the Leopards and Wolves tangle. Blount prevailed 21-13 and went on to capture the Class 5A state title. Vigor reached the Class 6A championship game that season but lost to Vestavia Hills.

VESTAVIA HILLS VS. HOOVER (BERRY)

Growing up in Thomasville in south Alabama, Buddy Anderson had no doubt about who the student body would cheer for during a pep rally. But as a young assistant coach at Vestavia Hills High, he got a startling revelation during the Rebels' pep rally for its first-ever game against neighboring Berry.

"Vestavia opened in 1970 and most of the kids who came to Vestavia had been going to Berry," Anderson said. "We opened the '72 season against Berry, and they had a good team. We had some players who had a choice that year to finish at Berry or Vestavia, and most of the good athletes stayed at Berry.

"We had a pep rally in the school auditorium. I'd been to a lot of pep rallies, and they had always been about school spirit, but that day half the students cheered for Vestavia and half cheered for Berry. I was blown away by that."

However, not as bad as he was blown away by the game. "They beat us 40-something to nothing," Anderson said. "They beat us every way you can be beaten. It was a rude awakening."

Because of the close proximity of the two schools, the rivalry intensified. "The kids knew each other, and many of them had gone to school together in elementary school," Anderson said.

"I remember the first time we beat them," he said. "We won 7-6, and it was a major feat. We didn't beat them again until 1980. We went to the finals in 1978, but they beat us 21-14."

Anderson took over as head coach in 1978 and formed a friendship with Berry head coach Bob Finley. "We had the utmost respect for each other, but we wanted to beat each other on Friday night," Anderson said with a hearty laugh.

Berry, which became Hoover High in 1994, dominated the rivalry in the 1970s, then it was Vestavia's turn in the 1980s and 1990s. At the turn of the century, the rivalry turned bitter with the arrival of Rush Propst as Hoover's head coach. The highly energetic and highly competitive Propst with his win-at-any-cost mentality rubbed the low-key Anderson the wrong way.

Hoover and Vestavia battle in the semifinals of the 2003 state playoffs.
Courtesy of Ed Tyler, prepsports.us

Plus, Hoover became the dominant football program in the state, winning five state championships in a six-season span from 2000-2005, including an unprecedented four consecutively for a Class 6A school.

In 2003, the teams' game was nationally televised on the Football Network, a network based in Chicago, and Vestavia Hills stunned Hoover 36-34 on the Rebels' home field. But the Bucs gained revenge with a 31-24 double-overtime victory in the semifinals of the playoffs en route to another state title.

GUNTERSVILLE VS. ALBERTVILLE

In 2004, before the 90th renewal of the state's oldest high school football rivalry, which dates to 1914, Guntersville Wildcats head coach Phil Isom expressed concern about facing the winless Albertville Aggies in the final game of the regular season.

"You can throw the records out with the Albertville-Guntersville game. Traditionally, it's always been a dogfight," Isom told the *Sand Mountain Reporter* before his Wildcats blistered the Aggies 39-7, sending Albertville to its first winless season (0-10) since 1970 when it finished 0-9-1.

Isom was right about one thing. Things haven't always been friendly in the series, which Albertville leads 44-41-6, despite losing 12 of the last 18 games through 2005. "I played in it for three years and coached in it for nine years," said Paul McAbee, who played and coached at Albertville and is the school's current principal. "It's always been an intense rivalry, but it's not as big as it was in the 1950s. It was usually played on Thanksgiving Day and there were a lot of fights.

"When I played, it was pretty bad. Back in 1971, there was a free-for-all. Players were fighting and both schools were put on probation [by the AHSAA]. There have been two or three incidents since then, but not like it was in the '50s. It was wild."

The series also had one loyal fan, "Mississippi" Bill Harris, who rooted for Guntersville. Harris witnessed 84 consecutive games in the rivalry, but died in August 2005, a few months before the Wildcats routed the Aggies 37-0.

"Bill would always come by before the game, and we always looked forward to seeing him," Isom said. "He was just a big part of the Albertville-Guntersville game."

BLACK HIGH SCHOOL RIVALRIES

Before integration, Blount's biggest rivals were a trio of black high schools from Mobile—Williamson, Toulminville (now LeFlore), and Central, where baseball great Hank Aaron played his first two years of high school and became an All-City guard in football.

The colorful Albert "Tipping" Terry coached both Williamson and Blount during his 34-year career and won a state title at Williamson.

Elsewhere in the state, some of the better rivalries among black schools were in Montgomery between Carver and Booker T. Washington and in Tuscaloosa between Druid and Riverside. The Druid-Riverside rivalry was bitter, according to Florzell Horton, who was a fullback at Druid from 1965-68 and later played for Marshall University.

"We played them every year on Thanksgiving Day," Horton said. "They called it the 'Battle of the Bridge,' because a bridge separated the two schools. If you got caught on their side of the bridge, you got beat up, and it was the same way on our side.

"It was the game you looked forward to every year. If you hadn't won any other game all year, you wanted to win that game. I remember one year they beat us by six points and a boy on our team dropped two touchdown passes. Our coach, Lou Mims, made him walk back home from school, while the rest of us rode the bus, and folks were throwing rocks at him."

Cobb Avenue of Anniston was on just about every black school's schedule because it was the only black school in the Anniston and had to travel throughout the state to play. In 1964, Cobb would have won the Alabama Interscholastic Athletic Association (AIAA) championship if it weren't for the Carver-Montgomery Wolverines. Cobb lost to Carver 19-0 to open the season but won the rest of its games to earn a rematch against the Wolverines, who had gone undefeated. But the rematch was worse than the first meeting for Cobb as Carver rolled to a 32-0 victory to claim the title.

Carver coach John Fulgham, who was inducted into the AHSAA Hall of Fame in 2004, was amazed at his team's performance in the championship game. "They were something else," Fulgham said of his players. "They really had strong feelings for each other, and they just didn't want to lose. Those were tough boys."

In Birmingham, there was the "Big 5" group of schools with the Parker Thundering Herd, Carver-Birmingham, Ullman, Western-Olin, and Hayes. Parker, led by AHSAA Hall of Fame coach Major Brown, was the dominant team and developed an intense rivalry with Ullman.

"Ullman played Parker hard," said Willie Scoggins, who played quarterback for the Herd in the 1940s. "They were from the other section of town and really wanted to beat us."

Parker also developed rivalries against schools outside the city such as Dunbar in Bessemer and Fairfield. "Those were threats," Scoggins said. And the Herd had out-of-state rivals, such as Booker T. Washington of Atlanta, Howard of Chattanooga, Tennessee, and Central of Louisville, Kentucky.

7

MEMORABLE GAMES AND PERFORMANCES

A CROWD LIKE NO OTHER

A week before the largest crowd—42,000-plus—to ever watch a high school football game in Alabama descended on Legion Field in Birmingham on November 8, 1974, Banks High head coach George "Shorty" White placed a call to the manager of the so-called "Football Capital of the South."

"I called him and told him if we stayed undefeated and Woodlawn stayed undefeated, we were going to have the biggest crowd we've ever had," White said. "I told him to treat it like a college game. He said there had never been a high school game they couldn't handle with just the front gate open."

The manager should have listened to White. The Banks Jets, featuring star quarterback Jeff Rutledge, entered the game 8-0, and the Woodlawn Colonels, featuring star running back Tony Nathan, also were 8-0. The winner would earn a berth to the state playoffs; the loser would be left at home in the postseason.

Fans throughout Birmingham and across the state flocked to Legion Field, so many in fact that the game had to be delayed twice—for more than 30 minutes—to let people into the stadium.

"There were more people outside the stadium than inside," Rutledge said. "People had talked all week about it being a big crowd."

"It was most electric situation I'd ever been in," said Dyer Carlisle, Banks' defensive coordinator who's now the principal at Homewood High School. "They didn't have enough gates open. They were taking up dollars and they ran out of change."

During the delay, the teams were in their locker rooms. "We had warmups, and then we went to the locker room," Rutledge said. "While the game was delayed, I remember sitting there being very nervous."

"We were in our locker room wondering why we couldn't go out and play," Nathan said. "We were getting upset. Our mindset was we were supposed to play at a certain time, so let's play. It's not our fault people can't get in."

Finally, White said he told the officials the players were getting cold and to start play.

"After we started, 20,000 people got back in their cars to go back home," White said. "It could have 60,000 in there if they had all the gates open."

Banks, which entered the game averaging 45 points per game, prevailed 18-7. Despite being sacked seven times, Rutledge completed nine-of-10 passes for 185 yards and a touchdown. Jets running back Jerry Murphree rushed for 99 yards on 14 carries and scored twice on runs of 21 and 16 yards.

"We played really well offensively and really well defensively," Rutledge said. "I threw one touchdown pass [of 32 yards] to Bob Grefseng, dragging across the middle, but the key was our defense. We had a guy named Greg Muse and he was isolated on Tony the whole game. That was one of the best games he ever played. Tony still got his yards, but he had to earn them."

Nathan rushed for 112 yards, but it took 31 carries, and he scored the Colonels' only touchdown on a 13-yard run midway through the fourth quarter.

The victory proved costly for Banks, which was trying to win its third consecutive state championship. "Woodlawn butchered us," White said. "We lost three defensive starters against them. It was a physical game. It was usually that way when we played them.

"We lost Rutledge to a broken ankle the next week against West End and lost that game. It's hard to come off a game as big as the game against Woodlawn was and beat a good opponent the next week."

Banks had a bye in the first round of the playoffs, but lost 12-0 to eventual champion Homewood in the next round.

"That Woodlawn team was the best team we played. If they had let them in the playoffs, they would have won [the state championship]— after we lost," White said.

Rutledge and Nathan wound up as teammates at the University of Alabama and led the Crimson Tide to a national championship in 1978, but Rutledge never brought up their memorable high school game.

"I can't ever remember us having a conversation about it," he said.

NATIONAL RECORDS WEREN'T ON RUSSELL GUNTER'S MIND

When Straughn High School took the field at Coffee Springs in week 10 of the 1986 season, senior running back Russell Gunter had some specific goals in mind.

He wanted a win to ensure the Bulldogs of their first winning season during his high school career. He wanted at least 100 yards rushing to put him over 2,000 yards on the season.

And he wanted to show college scouts he had what it would take to play football at the next level.

When the night was over, the 5-foot-11, 165-pound senior who wore No. 85, had reached two of those goals, but missed out on the one he

Russell Gunter. *Courtesy of AHSAA*

really wanted most. Gunter ran for 339 yards on 72 carries. That's right. Seventy-two carries.

The carries set a national record that still had not been seriously challenged 20 years later, but Coffee Springs came away with a 22-21 win—leaving Straughn with a 5-5 record.

"I knew I had carried the ball a lot," said Gunter, who played football in junior college at Mississippi Delta and later transferred to Troy State University where he walked on, then decided to concentrate on his degree. "I just had no idea it would be anything like a national record. I had gone over 50 carries a few times already that season. I set a state record with 53 against Jay, Florida. Running 50 times isn't so much different than running 72 times."

Gunter, who was an outstanding prep athlete despite having a 60-percent hearing loss, said the game was a wild one from the start. "We went 0-10 when I was a sophomore and 1-9 my junior year, but we were pretty excited about our senior year," said Gunter, who moved from end to running back in the middle of his junior year—hence the No. 85 jersey. "We had a lot of close games, and we lost some we shouldn't have. It cost us a chance at going to the state playoffs for the first time in school history."

The game was a contrast of styles. "We would grind it out with long drives," Gunter said. "Then we'd kick off and they would run the kickoff back. We got the ball back down by one with about nine minutes to play."

The plays weren't fancy: Gunter off right tackle; Gunter off left tackle. "We only had four real drives all night," he said. "I was running behind our fullback Mark Dewrell. I scored touchdowns on the first three drives. After Coffee Springs took the lead, we drove the length of the field and got the ball to the 4-yard line with enough time to run one more play.

"I just knew we would run me one more time. Instead, Coach called for a field-goal try. We missed and lost. I feel certain I had one more run left in me. I would have gotten the four yards."

Gunter didn't think about anything after the game except the loss—and how tired he really was. At one point in the game, he said, a fight broke out between the two teams. "I just sat down near midfield and just watched," he said. "I was too tuckered out to do anything else. I went home that night, and about all I remember before I fell asleep is that my mom gave my old legs a good rubdown. I was still sore the next day, but by noon I was helping my dad and brother harvest our peanut crop.

"Looking back on it, I guess it was a pretty special night. Folks came up to me after the game and told me what a great game I had played. It was bittersweet for me. I didn't realize just how big the 72 carries were at first. Later I learned that few teams ever get 72 plays in a game, much less one person. And while running the ball 72 times was pretty special,

I give the credit to our offensive line. Those guys had to block 72 times, too."

Gunter said his opponents that night were gracious in the end. "The players from Coffee Springs all shook my hand and told me how they admired how hard I had played. It just didn't seem all that much out of the ordinary back then."

Gunter finished the season with 426 rushing attempts—an Alabama state record for 10 games. He also finished with 2,220 yards.

He really wanted to continue playing football in college and signed with Mississippi Delta Junior College, but he grew homesick and eventually gave up the dream to help his dad on their Covington County farm. He got his degree by commuting more than 70 miles one way to Troy State each day. He graduated from Troy State in 1992 and began working at Eglin Air Force Base in Florida the very next week, where he has worked ever since. He is currently an Acquisition Program Manager working with Foreign Military Air Forces to integrate weapons systems on fighter planes. He travels around the world to meet with foreign customers.

He married his high school sweetheart, Leigh Ann Nichols. "She believes me when I tell her about the record," he said. "She has to. She saw the game."

MAC CAMPBELL DEFIES THE ODDS

When Demetrius "Mac" Campbell burst onto the Alabama prep sports scene in 1992, he was a small, but quick tailback who worked his way into Alexandria's starting lineup rushing for 1,200 yards.

By the time his career finally ended—in the winner's circle of the Class 4A state finals at Legion Field in 1997—Campbell had become the state's all-time leading rusher with 9,839 yards and the nation's record holder for career touchdowns with 153.

Ironically, none of those records mattered much to the incredible runner following the 1996 season. His team had just been beaten in the third round of the Class 4A state playoffs when Campbell was stricken with bacterial meningitis.

His battle moved from the football field to the intensive care unit of the University of Alabama-Birmingham Medical Center as he clung to his very life. "I was just trying to live," said Campbell. "Football wasn't important to me then. I was fighting for my life."

The 5-foot-10, 175-pound Campbell was unconscious for a week and remained hospitalized for almost a month. When he returned to school in January of 1997, he was physically weak and emotionally drained. Yet he was determined to get back on the field and lead the Valley Cubs to a state title his senior year.

"I had plenty of time to think about why the Lord spared me and let me survive the meningitis," Campbell said. "I know He has given me a special talent. And I know He expects me to use it to the best of my ability. I also know that football, although it is very important to me, isn't as precious to me as life itself."

During his senior season, Campbell rushed for 2,582 yards in 14 games as Coach Larry Ginn's Valley Cubs won the 4A state championship. Campbell scored 37 touchdowns that final season—all after recovering from the bout with meningitis. He was named MVP of Alexandria's 24-14 win over Greensboro in the Super Six Class 4A finals.

Campbell moved from Anniston to Alexandria in junior high. In high school, he became one of many special players who was well known by his nickname "Mac." His career was successful from the start. After gaining 1,200 yards and 15 touchdowns on 163 carries in 10 games as an eighth-grader, he became the Valley Cubs' workhorse as a freshman, rolling up 1,817 yards and 30 touchdowns on 246 carries as Alexandria reached the Class 4A playoffs. As a sophomore, he had the first of three consecutive 2,000-yard seasons, gaining 2,220 yards on 241 carries and scoring 35 touchdowns as Alexandria went 15-0 and won the state crown.

As a junior, Campbell piled up 2,006 yards and 36 TDs on 207 carries with his team reaching the quarterfinals of the 4A playoffs.

Prior to his team's playoff game with Fayette County, Campbell began to complain of headaches. He said the pain didn't ease off—but he failed to tell his coaches.

"Once the game started, I guess my adrenaline took over and I forgot about the pain," he later told reporters. The next day, he was at an uncle's house with his girlfriend when the pain overwhelmed him. He was taken to Anniston Regional Medical Center's emergency room and was about to be sent home when he threw up twice and then passed out. Almost a week later, he woke up in the ICU unit at UAB with tubes and electrodes attached to him.

"They tell me my heart stopped, and they had to revive it," Campbell said. "I don't remember any of that. I don't remember anything."

While he was in a coma, Alexandria coaches, teachers, and students kept vigil at UAB as prayer chains developed at schools across the state. Cards and letters began to roll in—from Fayette County's students and players, even from Alexandria's chief rival, Cleburne County.

Ginn said the family and school were overwhelmed by the concern shown by rival schools and students from across the state.

Once out of the hospital, Campbell was told by doctors to take it easy for a while and build his strength back up gradually. So he skipped basketball as a junior. Campbell was in the bleachers later in March at the Final Four when Alexandria teammate and friend Antwan Burton heaved the ball 65 feet at the buzzer to send the semifinal game with Daleville into overtime. The Valley Cubs won the game 98-96 and claimed the state title two days later.

Campbell's comeback started slowly. He had lost weight, was weak and out of shape in June. He didn't really begin to reach his peak until the third game of the season—when he ran for 248 yards on 21 carries and had three TDs in a 35-7 win over Butler. The next week, he broke the state TD record on his first carry versus Emma Sansom—going 80 yards for the 123rd TD of his career.

"I remember thinking to myself as I knelt down in the end zone, 'Thank you Lord. I'm back.'" He would score 30 more touchdowns before the season's conclusion.

That shot by Burton in the basketball tournament was called a "miracle shot" by those who saw it, but those close to Alexandria admitted it was just a game. The real miracle was sitting in the stands watching. And that same miracle was standing in the winner's circle the next December with a championship trophy to prove it.

"The entire saga with Mac was something as a coach you just don't forget," Ginn said. "Mac was a special kid here who has touched a lot of lives. Just having him still with us, having him alive and having him as part of the team was an answer to our prayers. I have never seen a player like him, a player so talented, yet so humble. We have been very blessed."

Now, that's a miracle.

TAKING THE FIFTH

When the Alabama High School Athletic Association instituted a state playoff system in 1966, it was determined that teams that played to a tie in championship games would be declared co-champions. Four times there were co-champs when the AHSAA had four classifications:

> 1971 – Class 2A – Abbeville 0, Oneonta 0
> 1976 – Class 3A – Andalusia 7, Athens 7
> 1979 – Class 3A – Jackson 0, Colbert County 0
> 1982 – Class 4A – Enterprise 10, Berry 10

In 1983, the AHSAA decided that tied championship games would be settled with overtime. That year Millport beat Brantley 3-0 in overtime to win the Class 1A championship. Six more overtime championship games followed over the years, but none lasted more than two overtimes.

> 1987 – Class 5A — Greenville 21, Russellville 20, (2 OT)
> 1990 – Class 4A — Deshler 28, T.R. Miller 27
> 1996 – Class 3A — Colbert County 25, UMS-Wright 19 (2 OT)
> 1997 – Class 3A — Aliceville 21, Colbert County 19
> 1998 – Class 5A — Blount 27, Etowah 20
> 1999 – Class 6A — Clay-Chalkville 30, Lee-Montgomery 27

Then, in 2000, there was the most dramatic championship game ever played. The Homewood Patriots defeated the Benjamin Russell Wildcats 41-34 in a record-setting five overtimes to claim the Class 5A title in the Super 6 Championships at Legion Field.

Benjamin Russell held a 10-0 lead until the final quarter when Homewood quarterback Parker Gargis scored on a 1-yard run. Jeremy Schatz' 33-yard field goal, following a Benjamin Russell fumble, brought Homewood even. Regulation play ended with a 10-10 score when Schatz' 27-yard field goal attempt was blocked by Eric Brock with eight seconds left.

Overtime rules in Alabama high school football have the captains of the two teams meet in the middle of the field for a coin toss, and then each team gets the ball at the 10-yard line with four plays to score.

Homewood 41, Benjamin Russell 34, 5 OT										
Homewood	0	0	0	10	7	7	7	3	7	41
Benjamin Russell	7	0	3	0	7	7	7	3	0	34

Scoring summary

First quarter

BR -- Jewonski Kendrick 1 yd run (Brent Dye kick) 00:03

Third quarter

BR – Dye 24 field goal 2:10

Fourth quarter

H – Parker Gargis 1 yd run (Jeremy Schatz kick) 10:35

H – Schatz 33 field goal 8:53

Overtime

H – Jake Collins 5 yd pass from Gargis (Schatz kick)

BR – Thomas Jordan 7 yd run (Dye kick)

BR – Kendrick 1 yd run (Dye kick)

H – Gargis 4 yd run (Schatz kick)

H – Gargis 5 yd run (Schatz kick)

BR – Kendrick 2 yd run (Dye kick)

BR – Dye 34 field goal

H – Schatz 23 field goal

H – Colt Byrom 5 yd pass from Gargis (Schatz kick)

In overtime, the Patriots and Wildcats erupted for a combined 55 points and matched point totals in each extra period until the fifth one. Homewood scored first on a 5-yard touchdown pass from Gargis to senior receiver Colt Byrom. Then, on Benjamin Russell's possession, Jordan Thomas' fourth-and-six pass attempt was knocked down in the end zone by Homewood defensive back Jonathan Herr to end the marathon game.

"It seemed like this was never going to end," Homewood head coach Bob Newton said, while looking at his watch. It took forever, but it was worth it."

Jewonski Kendrick scored three touchdowns, two in overtime, for Benjamin Russell.

Gargis was selected the game's MVP after rushing for 118 yards three touchdowns on 29 carries and completing 14-of-23 passes for 109 yards and two scores. "That was the longest game I have ever been a part of in my life," Gargis said. "I did not think it was going to end."

Five years later, at a championship flag-raising ceremony at Homewood's Waldrop Stadium, Byrom reflected on the incredible ending. "I think about that game all the time," Byrom said. "I watch video of it from time to time. On the sidelines we were never able to relax, and after we won it, it was unbelievable. There was tons of excitement, but we were drained emotionally and physically. I feel so lucky to have been a part of that game."

A NIGHT TO REMEMBER: JACK GOLSON'S 55-POINT EFFORT

In 1950, daring return specialists were an unheard-of commodity. That is, everywhere perhaps except Fort Deposit, Alabama. Coach Fred Taylor struck gold in senior receiver and halfback Jack Golson. The speedster, whose dad, Carl Golson, owned the local Cadillac dealership, might well have been the original "Cadillac" in prep football circles. In the season of 1950, he and fellow senior teammate Jack McDonald set the recruiting world on fire with their long-play exploits in an 8-1 season for Lowndes County High School.

For Golson, no night was bigger than the early November date with Loretto High School. He scored a then-national-record 55 points that night—running back five punts for touchdowns, one kickoff for a score, two runs for TDs, and kicking seven extra points in the 61-13 win.

First, though, take a look at the "two Jacks" heading up to that night. In game one of the season, a 53-0 rout of McKenzie, Jack McDonald, the single-wing tailback, scored five touchdowns, and Jack Golson had the other three. Golson had a 40-yard TD pass from McDonald and returned two interceptions for scores. The next week, Georgiana did something no other opponent could do the rest of the year—keeping both Jacks out of the end zone in a 19-7 win over Lowndes County.

It was back to business as usual the next week, a 48-13 win over Starke Academy. Golson and McDonald scored three touchdowns each. A 39-13 win over Excel was highlighted the next week by Golson's 30-yard TD run and 65-yard kickoff return for a score.

A 40-0 win over Ramer made Lowndes County 4-1 on the year. McDonald had three touchdowns, including a 70-yard scoring run, and Golson hauled in a 70-yard TD pass from his buddy. Lowndes County (4-1) beat a tough Luverne team 34-2 the next week as Golson had what would be a career night for most players. He caught three TD passes from McDonald covering 41, 90, and 31 yards. McDonald also scored twice on runs of 53 and 4 yards.

A 52-12 rout of Hicks Memorial from nearby Autaugaville included two TD pass receptions by Golson and a 90-yard kickoff return for a score. McDonald scored four TDs and passed for two.

Next came Loretto. Golson returned four punts for scores in the first quarter on returns of 65, 50, 90, and 75 yards. He added a 75-yard kickoff return and 73-yard punt return for two more scores and tacked on runs of 20 and 30 yards for touchdowns in the 61-13 triumph.

His 55 points and eight TDs were state records. The eight-TD mark went unequaled for 47 years—when Golinsky Smith of Sylacauga tied the mark with eight TDs in a 70-35 win over Chelsea. John Tucker tied the mark in 1998 for Frisco City in a 51-20 win over Sweet Water.

Tony Dixon of Parrish also tied the eight-TD record in 2003 and also broke Golson's record of 55 points scored overall with 57 in the Tornadoes' 81-58 win over Hubbertville in 2003. Dixon had eight touchdowns and nine extra points.

Golson's 430 return yards—an average of 71.7 yards per return—was still a national record after the 2005 season.

Golson's astounding season ended with him scoring three more touchdowns, including a 60-yard punt return and receptions of 9 and 25 yards as Lowndes County downed rival Hayneville 27-0.

For the year, Golson had 12 pass receptions, seven punt returns, and three kickoff returns for touchdowns and had 26 TDs total. He also kicked 37 extra points and finished with 199 points.

At the school's season-ending football banquet in Fort Deposit, at least six southern college head coaches attended. Jack Golson received the Carl Golson Sportsmanship Award and the team was the recipient of the Central Alabama Football Officials Association Sportsmanship Award.

Golson and McDonald were both named All-State for their efforts.

AMAZING COMEBACK:
HAZLEWOOD 17-CORDOVA 14 (OT) 1988

Hazlewood's Golden Bears were staring at defeat in the semifinals of the 1988 state playoffs when the most amazing last five seconds in AHSAA state history set into motion the first of five consecutive Class 2A state championships for the Tornadoes.

Cordova's powerful Blue Devils were leading 14-6 at Hudson-Kirby Stadium in this coal-mining community just west of Jasper and had the ball with only 30 seconds remaining.

Coach Tim O'Neil's team had the ball on their 10-yard line and was facing fourth down. He watched as the clock ticked down to just five seconds before a flag was thrown for delay of game. A timeout was called so Cordova could make sure they knew exactly what their coach wanted them to do on what should have been the final play.

During the time out, O'Neil instructed his team to line up in punt formation and told his punter to take the snap, run around in the end zone until time expired, and then kneel down or step out of the end zone for a safety. With no time remaining, his team would waltz into the finals at New Brockton the next week with a 14-8 victory.

The Blue Devils had shut down Hazlewood's powerful offense all night—yielding only a 99-yard kickoff return for a touchdown to start the second half to Bears junior Antonio Langham. The last thing O'Neil said he wanted to do was kick the ball away to Langham, always a threat to score when he touched the ball.

After the timeout, however, O'Neil noticed something he didn't expect. Langham didn't line up deep to receive the punt. Instead, he lined up on the outside as a rusher.

Cordova's coach then changed his mind. A pooch kick just over the defense's head could be downed before a defender could get to the ball. "Seemed like the safest play," O'Neil reasoned. He had no way of knowing that Langham would be a future SEC star at Alabama and a first-round NFL draft pick of the Cleveland Browns. He soon found out, however.

"What happened next is the most amazing thing I have ever seen in football," said Clyde Goode Sr., the uncle of Antonio Langham. "You have to understand, I don't think anyone in that stadium thought Hazlewood had a chance to win—other than the Hazlewood players on the field."

During the timeout, the Bears had received some added incentive when the public address announcer asked any Cordova fans wishing to ride a charter bus to the state finals the next week at New Brockton to meet outside the stadium behind the press box after the game.

The players were on the field waiting for Cordova to return when the announcement was made, said Goode. "They all looked toward to the press box and pointed to the five seconds still remaining on the clock," he said.

When the ball was whistled into play, Langham streaked from his outside end position to block the punt attempt in the end zone. He recovered for a touchdown as the final horn sounded.

Hazlewood then went to Langham for a two-point conversion to tie the score.

To break ties in Alabama high school football, the teams' captains meet in the middle of the field and flip a coin, and then each team gets the ball at the 10-yard line with four plays to score. A turnover ends a team's possession.

Cordova lost the coin toss and got the ball first, but fumbled when Langham jarred the ball loose from a Blue Devils runner, and the Bears recovered. Hazlewood then lined up as Langham booted a field goal to give the Bears a 17-14 victory as a stunned and packed stadium looked on in silence.

The next week, Hazlewood rolled over New Brockton 28-0 to win the state title—starting the Bears on an unprecedented seven-year run that produced five straight 2A championships and two runner-up finishes.

GETTING IN HIS KICKS

Playing in a B-team game as a freshman at Huffman High School in Birmingham, Philip Doyle lined up to attempt a 48-yard field goal. The officials were so sure he couldn't kick the ball that distance that they didn't bother to position themselves under the goal post. When the ball sailed through the uprights, one of the officials leaped into the air in amazement and raised his arms high to signal the kick good.

Doyle had played soccer when the sport was just beginning to gain a foothold in the state. "I was about six years old and I started playing soccer at Franklin Academy, a little private school," Doyle recalled. "About two years before I was going to start high school, I played metro football for the 115-pound Huffman Raiders. They needed a kicker, and I said maybe I'll try. I played soccer and learned to kick, but I never expected to be a kicker. In the eighth grade, I was kicking field goals 40-45 yards, so I knew I could excel."

By the time he was a junior in 1985, no one was surprised to see Doyle jog onto the field to attempt a field goal. That season he set a national record for field goals in a single season with 22 (in 27

Huffman placekicker Phillip Doyle kicks a field goal. *Courtesy Birmingham Post-Herald*

attempts). Doyle made six field goals longer than 45 yards, including one of 51 yards.

"When the season was over, I looked at the stats, and it shocked me that I had so many over 40 yards," he said. "We didn't think anything about me going out there to kick field goals my junior and senior year."

By the time Doyle finished his high school career he had established a national record for field goals made in a career with 43 (in 55 attempts).

WORKING OVERTIME

When Etowah (9-1) met Oxford (7-4) in the first round of the AHSAA Class 5A state playoffs in November of 1991, little did the fans and players realize just what was in store.

The two bitter rivals battled to a 28-28 tie through four regulation quarters, but by the time the game had ended some 90 minutes later, Etowah had come away with a wild 69-63 victory that took six overtimes.

The game set several records—the one foremost was Oxford's 63 points in the loss. At the time, it was the most points ever scored in a prep football game by the losing team. The 76 points scored in overtime were also a record for two teams.

Oxford came in the decided underdog. Etowah was one of the state's top teams with the state's top quarterback prospect, Freddy Kitchens, at the throttles. Kitchens, a husky 6-foot-4, 230-pound gunslinger who had college recruiters and professional baseball scouts evaluating his arm nightly, was a likely hero on this cold night.

It was Kitchens' strong legs that finally ended the marathon. He scored the deciding touchdown on a 3-yard keeper as the clock approached midnight.

In the AHSAA by 1991, teams were forbidden to have a game end in a tie—especially in the playoffs. The passing tandem of Kitchens and Toderick Malone—both of whom wound up wearing the Crimson jersey of the University of Alabama in college—were sensational. Kitchens fired five TD passes. Malone caught three.

Oxford quarterback Galen Sprayberry was almost as effective for the Yellow Jackets. He passed for four TDs and rushed for another. Oxford place-kicker Clyde Abernathy also kicked nine extra points.

The overtime procedure used in Alabama was simple. Each team would get four offensive plays from the 10-yard line. If the score remained tied following the two possessions, then another overtime would begin at the 10. After every two overtimes, the captains and officials would flip a coin to choose which team got first possession.

A turnover could be deadly in overtime—especially if the other team scored first.

In the first extra period, Etowah got the ball first and took a 35-28 lead when Dominick Pinson scored on a 10-yard run. Oxford countered with Chris Cunningham sprinting in from the 8 and Abernathy kicking the extra point.

In the second overtime, Keith Bargerhuff scored for Oxford on a 7-yard pass from Sprayberry. Abernathy's kick made it 42-35. The Jackets defense stiffened on the Blue Devils' possession. Facing a fourth-and-goal from the 5, Malone took a reverse handoff from Kitchens and scored around the end, and the kick tied the game again.

In the third overtime, Kitchens scored on a 6-yard run, and Charles Wright, who had three TD receptions, caught a fourth-and-10 pass from Sprayberry with a dramatic leaping catch to tie the game at 49 all.

None of the fans had left Etowah's Glover Stadium when the fourth overtime began. Oxford's Kirk Barker found a seam in the tiring Blue Devils defense for a 4-yard TD run. Kitchens quickly found Todd Lamberth for a 10-yard scoring strike to make it 56-56.

In the fifth overtime, Etowah got the ball first and lost eight yards on two plays back to the 18-yard line. Facing a third-and-long situation, Kitchens found his favorite target Malone on a beautiful comeback pass in the end zone to make it 63-56. Oxford wasn't through, however. Sprayberry sneaked in from the 2 to tie the game again.

In the sixth overtime, Oxford was finally running out of gas. On fourth-and-two, linebacker Brent Kulavich blitzed through the Jackets line to sack Sprayberry short of the end zone.

All Etowah had to do was kick a field goal to win. However, the Blue Devils elected to try to score the touchdown after Pinson streaked nine yards to the 1 on first down. An illegal procedure penalty on second down moved Etowah back to the 6. Pinson got three yards to the 3, and Kitchens then ended it all with a strong 3-yard keeper into the end zone.

"I don't think I have ever been so tired," said Kitchens after the game. "And I don't think I had ever been so thrilled to win a game. It was something none of us will ever forget."

That playoff game, which was one shy of the state record of seven overtimes played in Murphy's 34-31 win over Theodore in 1979, has stood the test of time as the most exciting OT game in state history as the two teams piled up almost 1,000 yards between them.

Only Homewood's five-overtime 41-34 win over Benjamin Russell in the Class 5A finals in the 2000 Super 6 at Legion Field in

Birmingham—televised statewide live on TV—has come close to capturing that intense excitement.

A "DULL" 125-0 AFFAIR

Little is known about the biggest shutout in the history of Alabama high school football. It happened in 1925 when neighboring Chambers County rivals Langdale and Milltown clashed. Talk about running up the score, Langdale won 125-0, scoring 19 touchdowns and 11 extra points on dropkicks by Hubert Wilkerson.

In a newspaper account of the contest, the reporter wrote that the "game was too dull to describe in detail."

Langdale no longer exists. The school was consolidated out of existence not many years after the "dull," but historic game. The city ceased to exist in 1980 when the towns of Langdale, Riverview, Fairfax, and Shawmut, the so-called "mill villages," voted to incorporate into the city of Valley near the Alabama-Georgia state line.

Although the city of Milltown is still around, the school isn't. The public school students there attend Lafayette High.

8

MISCELLANEOUS/ ANECDOTES

ENCOUNTERS WITH BEAR AND SHUG

Although legendary Alabama football coach Paul "Bear" Bryant didn't play or coach high school football in Alabama, he still had a dramatic impact on prep football in the state. Take for the instance the time he came to Birmingham in 1982 to visit Ensley senior football player Cornelius Bennett.

Steve Savarese was Ensley's head football coach then, and Bryant's visit left him red-faced.

"Coach Bryant is the reason I got into coaching," Savarese said. "He was an inspiration to me when I was at Leeds High School. He was someone who is bigger than life. When I was a young coach, I got to be around him. The first time I ever met Coach Bryant was in his office at a coaching clinic, and he was sitting there eating fried chicken. I was afraid to say anything to him.

"Then, when I was at Ensley, he was recruiting Cornelius Bennett and was coming for a visit at the school. He was supposed to be there at 5 [p.m.] [Assistant] Coach [Ken] Donahue, who seemed so scared of

Coach Bryant, told me was always an hour early. If he said, 'If he tells you 5, he'll be there at 4.'

"I didn't think much about it. After school, I went out to run with Coach [Jimmy] Tucker and when I got back, I took a shower. When I came out of the shower, there was a knock on the door. I thought it was one of our other coaches, so I told them to come it. It was Coach Bryant and I was standing there butt naked. He said, 'Coach, did I come at a bad time? Do I need to step outside?' I didn't know what to say. I told him he was all right."

Savarese got dressed and told Bryant that Bennett had gone home and they could go up to his house. Then Bryant surprised Savarese again.

"Coach Bryant always made you feel comfortable, but when we got ready to go to Cornelius' house, he said, 'Coach, let's take your car,'" Savarese said. "He had a limo and his driver, Billy Varner, was with him. I was driving a little Volkswagen at the time and I said, 'Coach, are you sure? You might not be comfortable in my little car.' He said, 'I'll be all right. C'mon, let's take your car.'

"We drove to Cornelius' house and I'll never forget when Coach Bryant got out of the car, people started coming out of their houses to get a look at him."

Bryant also surprised Spence McCracken in his first year as a head coach at Montgomery Academy. McCracken's starting quarterback was Mark Tyson, who was Bryant's grandson. Bear made sure McCracken knew it, calling him into his office during a coaching clinic in Tuscaloosa.

"I was head coach at Montgomery Academy in 1979, and that was the first time I had a private conversation with Coach Bryant," McCracken recalled. "Everybody wanted to be like him. He sent [then assistant coach] Mal Moore down, and he told me Coach Bryant wanted to see me in his office. I didn't know for what. I was a little nervous when I walked into his office and he said, 'You know you're coaching my grandson,' and I said, 'Yeah, I got him out there. I think he's a good one.' He said, 'Don't let him get hurt.'"

McCracken felt a little threatened until Bryant added, "He's my fishing and hunting buddy." A relieved McCracken replied, "I'll try not to let him get hurt."

"I made sure I didn't let him get hurt," McCracken continued. "He played quarterback for me for two years, and Coach Bryant would come down to watch us practice, but he'd hide behind the stands so nobody could see him. I think he also came to a few of our games."

McCracken, who now coaches at Opelika High, also spent some time in the presence of Ralph "Shug" Jordan, playing for the legendary Auburn coach in the late 1960s.

Jordan played center in high school in Selma and in college at Auburn, and was also a long-snapper, the same positions McCracken played.

"Coach Jordan was like a father to me," McCracken said. "My dad died while I was in college, and he looked out for me. I kind of put him on a pedestal. I remember one time I had some money stolen, and one of the assistants told me to go see Coach Jordan and I got reimbursed.

"He was a great, great man. He taught us to fight and have courage. I didn't say many things to him, and Coach Jordan didn't say anything unless he had something to say. He was from the old school, hard-nosed. I think I'm an old-school guy, and I think I got that from him."

LONG BALLS INSTEAD OF FOOTBALL

Long before Hank Aaron supplanted Babe Ruth as baseball's home-run king, he was an offensive lineman, and a pretty good one at that.

Aaron played football for Central High School in Mobile and was All-City as a guard. But after his standout season, he gave up football because he was afraid he would get hurt and ruin his future in baseball.

It turned out to be the right decision.

Willie Mays, whom many thought would be the one to surpass Ruth's home-run record, also played football as a quarterback. In fact, Mays called football his first love. But, like Aaron, he quit the sport for fear of injury.

"At 15 I was playing professional ball with the Birmingham Black Barons, so I really came quickly in all sports," Mays said in an interview with the Academy of Achievement. "Basketball was my second sport. Football was my first, baseball was my last. But I picked baseball because it was the easiest of the three. And I don't think I had a problem with that, but the others I thought I would get hurt, so I just picked that. And my father didn't have money for me to go to college. And at that particular time they didn't have black quarterbacks, and I don't think I could have made it in basketball, because I was only 5-11. So I just picked baseball. There wasn't a height limit in baseball. You'd just go in and play and have a good time."

For Mays, like Aaron, it was the right choice.

PLAYOFF SPOT DECIDED BY ALABAMA SUPREME COURT RULING

When the first round of the Alabama High School Athletic Association state football playoffs rolled around in 1984, the game plan for Cordova and Phil Campbell high schools was being drawn up by lawyers—not coaches.

By week's end, a precedent had been set by the Alabama Supreme Court that has stood the test of time since.

It all stemmed from a court suit filed in Walker County Circuit Court by Cordova, a small Class 3A school in a western Walker County coal-mining community. The suit sought to overturn Phil Campbell's 25-24 regular-season victory over the Blue Devils played October 5. That loss kept the Blue Devils (9-1) from securing a state playoff berth and put the Bobcats (8-2), a small school located in Franklin County, in.

It culminated more than five weeks of bantering between school officials and the AHSAA's own appeals process, and even prompted Cordova fans to raise money for lawyers' fees by passing the hat at home games.

The controversy started during the sixth week of the season with unbeaten Cordova leading Phil Campbell 24-19 after scoring the go-ahead touchdown with 24 seconds remaining in the wild, flag-filled contest at Cordova's Hudson-Kirby Stadium.

Following the kickoff, Phil Campbell coach Mike Tice hurried his offense onto the field—sending out three receivers. On the first play, the Bobcats completed a touchdown pass to a receiver who had been lined up outside the line judge. He was standing all alone on the Phil Campbell sidelines, caught the ball, and sped untouched into the end zone for the winning TD.

Cordova coach Tim O'Neil argued the play was the deceptive "layout pass," in which a player steps onto the field after another runs off in an effort to deceive the defense. Because the player never went inside the line judge and within the required 15 yards of the line of scrimmage, then the play was illegal, he said.

No flag was thrown, however, and the TD counted.

Things didn't end there. With two seconds remaining, Phil Campbell kicked off to Cordova and was flagged for piling on during the ensuing return. Since the game couldn't end on a penalty, 15 yards were marked off, which set up Cordova with a chance for a winning field goal. The kick was good for an apparent 27-25 victory, but another flag was thrown—this time on the Blue Devils—for having only six players on the line of scrimmage. After backing up five yards, the second kick came up just short, and Phil Campbell won. Or so they thought.

When the regular season ended, Cordova had missed the playoffs because of the loss, and Phil Campbell had gotten in and had earned a first-round game against Lamar County of Vernon.

Cordova first went to AHSAA executive director Herman L. "Bubba" Scott to protest the final outcome. He denied the protest—emphasizing that he had never accepted a protest based on an official's call on the field and never would. The school then asked the AHSAA's Fifth District Legislative Council to throw out the final outcome and let the two teams replay the final 24 seconds or replay the game in its entirety.

The council denied the appeal. The AHSAA's Central Board of Control then heard the appeal and also denied the request. That's when the school took its plea to Walker County Circuit Judge Horace Nation

III by filing suit against the AHSAA, the officials involved, and Phil Campbell High School, asking the outcome be reversed.

On the day before the playoffs were set to start, Nation became the first judge in state history—and according to AHSAA lawyers, the first in the nation—to reverse the final outcome of an athletic contest because of a game official's action. A crowd of more than 150 players, parents, and fans gathered at the school's stadium to hear the news when the decision was first handed down.

Phil Campbell High School immediately filed suit in Franklin County Circuit Court, and Judge John Jolly issued a conflicting decision when he declared the AHSAA was "authorized to conduct the high school football championship program in the state of Alabama and should be allowed to determine which teams should be permitted to play" and the outcome be allowed to stay as is.

On the day of the game, Alabama's highest court then struck down both circuit judge decisions—and gave the deciding power back to the AHSAA—in effect returning Phil Campbell to the state playoffs.

Meanwhile, Lamar County High School had been studying film of both opponents all week. And as late as lunch on Friday, still wasn't sure which opponent would show up.

That night, Lamar County went out and did what all of Cordova's appeals couldn't do. The Bulldogs ousted Phil Campbell from the Class 3A state playoffs with a 42-7 win.

Four weeks later, Coach Kenneth McKinney's Bulldogs were crowned Class 3A state champions—going from 1-10 in 1983 to 13-1 with a 29-0 win over Randolph County in the finals. That dramatic turnaround, however, was forever overshadowed by the game that was eventually played out—not on a football field, but in the state's highest court.

AN AMERICAN IDOL

Ruben Studdard earned the nickname the "Velvet Teddy Bear" because of his soulful voice while becoming the 2003 American Idol and receiving the singing contract that came with it in the Fox reality TV program.

Curtis Coleman believes Studdard could have become a football "idol" if he had elected to stick with the gridiron instead of music. Studdard was an offensive lineman under Coach Coleman at Birmingham's Huffman High in the late 1990s.

"He was a good player, a really good player," Coleman said. "He worked extremely hard and he had a good attitude. He was an offensive right tackle, a great blocker. He was big and athletic. If he got into you, it could get ugly. He could put you away.

"He signed a football scholarship with Alabama A&M. I think he could have been a good college player, but he decided to give it up because his heart was always in music. When I heard he had given up on football to pursue music, I was upset because I thought he could do both."

Studdard sang in the school choir at Huffman, and Coleman noticed how much he enjoyed it. "When he sang, you could tell he loved doing it," Coleman said. "You knew he would be special because he had determination and he was going to do something big. I was not surprised he won the American Idol. He has a great attitude, a great personality."

IT AIN'T OVER UNTIL ... THE REFS SAY SO

Eufaula's Tigers found out the hard way in 1986. Coach Wayne Woodham's team left the field with a 21-19 victory at nearby Hardaway High School in Columbus, Georgia.

Woodham explained what happened next. "We were leading 21-19 with less than 30 seconds to play," he said. "I was told by an official that we had one timeout left, and Hardaway had none. Hardaway threw one incomplete pass in the end zone, then ran a play up the middle to our 8-yard line as time ran out as they were trying to get set to run another play."

Woodham said he walked to the middle of the field to shake the hand of Hardaway coach John Drew, but his adversary was busy cornering official B.R. Johnson near the 10-yard line.

He knew something was up, so he got his kids' attention in the middle of their victory celebration and ran off the field to the dressing room. As fate would have it, the visitors' dressing room was locked. Woodham was informed that Drew felt he had one timeout remaining. He said he had been told by an official on his side of the field that he had one more timeout left when he decided to run the ball one last time to try to set up a better angle for the field goal. He had the kicking tee in his hand when the official wound the clock following that play with eight seconds remaining. He said he had already started onto the field to talk to his team in what he thought was a granted timeout when he realized the clock was ticking down.

Woodham said his team was already getting undressed when he was informed the host team had been granted a timeout after all.

"We began taking our shoulder pads off and removing the tape from our ankles as we waited for the key to get into the dressing room," he said. "That's when I was told we had to go back out onto the field because Hardaway was given a timeout."

Woodham, in his first year as head coach after a long, successful stint at Greenville High School, almost decided to continue undressing and also wanted to argue his own case, but remembered that Eufaula's basketball team had a problem the year before and the school had been placed on probation.

After a delay of more than 15 minutes, the Tigers were ordered back onto the field. Hardaway then kicked the winning field goal for a 22-21 win.

"We felt we had won the game," Woodham said. "Our school board, city council, the whole city was up in arms about this. The chains had already been rolled up, for goodness sakes. I think the officials made a big mistake."

Drew insisted he requested the timeout before time expired. "Not granting a timeout when a team still has one is a correctable error," Drew said. "We think we won the game fair and square."

Hardaway might have won the game, but the controversy ended the series between the Alabama and Georgia high schools.

BIG FOOT

When Willie Anderson came out of Vigor High School in Prichard as the No. 1 college prospect in the state in 1992, it's a safe bet to say he hadn't heard of the song "Your Feet's Too Big" from Fats Waller's play "Ain't Misbehavin'."

Anderson could have starred in that role because at the time he was a 6-foot-7, 310-pound behemoth of an offensive tackle who stomped on foes with his big feet. Harold Clark, Anderson's high school coach, said that's partly what made him such an outstanding player for the Wolves. "He wears 19-1/2 shoes," Clark said. "People don't want to get stepped on."

Clark had difficulty finding shoes for Anderson because of his big feet. "I called all over the place," Clark said. "I called Alabama, Auburn, Texas, and nobody had them. You can't find them without getting them specially made. He's got the biggest shoe I ever saw. I don't see how he runs in those things."

Anderson didn't let his big feet trip him up. He ran the 40-yard dash in 4.9 seconds while at Vigor and also played on the Wolves' basketball team, and his junior season he led the Mobile area in rebounding.

Anderson took his big feet to Auburn and later to the NFL, where he's had a long career with the Cincinnati Bengals.

NUMBER 22 IS SAFE BET

For more than 30 years, a Smothers wore the No. 22 at Addison High School. That number also produced more coaches—thanks to the dedication of the Smothers boys.

Mark, Steve, Stan, and Micah, and grandsons Woody, David, Seth, and Benjamin Smothers have all donned that special number at one time or another through the years.

Steve, Mark, Micah, Woody, and David all went into high school coaching.

The family and the No. 22 are important in Addison lore.

Former Addison head coach Allen Stephenson, who guided the Bulldogs to the state 1A championship in 1976, said no one ever

Quarterback-linebacker Jake Gilliland dons the school's familiar No. 22 jersey while leading Addison to the 2005 Class 1A championship.
Courtesy of Ed Tyler, prepsports.us

thought about anyone wearing No. 22 outside the Smothers clan. "This family has just been too important to our community. They're really good folks," he said.

The Bulldogs had been in the state playoffs 23 times in the last 36 years, compiling a 43-23 playoff record after the 2005 state championship. The 1970 and 1976 teams won state titles. The 1971, 1975, and 1994 teams finished as state runner-up.

AT THE MOVIES

Hollywood has always had a certain fascination with athletes—and with Southerners. Alabama's high schools have been a breeding ground for screen stars.

Among them was western cowboy star Johnny Mack Brown. Brown was a real southerner, born in Dothan in 1904. Johnny Mack, the second of nine children, became a high school football star at Dothan High School, graduating in 1922.

The exciting running back went on to earn All-America honors at the University of Alabama and was one of the stars of the game when the Crimson Tide beat Washington in the 1926 Rose Bowl at Pasadena, California. Brown had three touchdowns in the game, and Hollywood was so enamored with Brown that he returned to California after graduation and a brief coaching stint, and became a hit of the silver screen.

He went to Hollywood and began doing bit parts around 1927 in the silent movies. Very handsome, he quickly became a leading man working opposite such screen bombshells as Mary Pickford, Greta Garbo, and Joan Crawford. His first big success was likely MGM's *Billy The Kid* (1930).

He went on to appear in 165 films during a career that spanned more than 40 years and with such studios as MGM, Universal, and Monogram. Old-time Western buffs know the answer to an obvious trivia question. What was the name of his horse?

Why, it was aptly named "Rebel," perfect for the Alabama-born Southern gentleman. Brown was also inducted into the College Football Hall of Fame in 1957 and the Rose Bowl Hall of Fame in 2001.

Buck Buchanan of Birmingham burst onto the screen in Super Bowl I when he recorded the first sack in Super Bowl history by sacking another Alabama-born native, Bart Starr of Montgomery. Both men would later be inducted into the Pro Football Hall of Fame.

Buchanan would also delve into acting with a role as a football star in Korea in the original movie *M*A*S*H* (1970).

While Richmond Flowers Jr., didn't star in the 1989 movie *Unconquered*, it was based on the former Alabama prep football and track phenom's family during the Civil Rights movement of the 1960s.

Young Flowers, who went on to star at the University of Tennessee and then played briefly with the Dallas Cowboys, was the fastest school

The Heisman voting and Alabama's high school connections				
Year	Player	College	Hometown	Rank in voting
1937	Joe Kilgrow	Alabama	Montgomery	5th
1945	Harry Gilmer	Alabama	Birmingham	5th
1946	Harry Gilmer	Alabama	Birmingham	7th
1947	Harry Gilmer	Alabama	Birmingham	5th
1957	Jim Phillips	Auburn	Alexander City	6th
1960	Ed Dyas	Auburn	Mobile	4th
1961	Pat Trammell	Alabama	Scottsboro	5th
1962	Lee Roy Jordan	Alabama	Excel	4th
1963	Jimmy Sidle	Auburn	Birmingham	7th
1968	Ron Sellers	Florida St.	Headland	10th
1970	Pat Sullivan	Auburn	Birmingham	6th
1971	Pat Sullivan	Auburn	Birmingham	Winner
1971	Johnny Musso	Alabama	Birmingham	4th
1979	Steadman Shealy	Alabama	Birmingham	10th
1983	Walter Lewis	Alabama	Brewton	9th
1985	Bo Jackson	Auburn	Bessemer	Winner
1986	Cornelius Bennett	Alabama	Birmingham	7th
1987	Bobby Humphrey	Alabama	Birmingham	10th
1993	David Palmer	Alabama	Birmingham	3rd
1994	Jay Barker	Alabama	Trussville	5th
2003	Philip Rivers	N.C. State	Athens	7th

boy in the nation in the high hurdles when he was at Sidney Lanier in Montgomery. His son, Richmond III, also played in the NFL and son Bill was the favorite target of Eli Manning at Ole Miss. Richmond III attended Vestavia Hills High School, and Bill played at Pelham.

Durmot McElroney played Richmond Jr., in the movie based on Flowers' dad, Richmond, Sr., and his unpopular pro-integration stance in Alabama in the 1960s. Peter Coyote played the dad. Richmond Jr., was not popular in high school due to the politics of the times.

Coach Bill Yoast was a key figure in *Remember The Titans*, the 2000 film about the integration of T.C. Williams High School in Richmond, Virginia, and its march to the state championship. Yoast was the white coach who moved from head coach to assistant when black coach Herman Boone took over. Yoast, played by Will Patton, grew up in Florence, Alabama, and went to Florence High School. Denzel Washington played Coach Boone in what has turned out to be one of the most popular sports movies of all time.

Lucas Black never won a state championship while prepping at Speake High School in Lawrence County, but he helped the Bobcats' basketball team reach the Northwest Regional finals when he was a junior.

He did, however, play Mike Winchell, the quarterback of the 1988 Odessa, Texas-Permian Panthers in the highly acclaimed *Friday Night Lights*, a 2004 film based on H.G. Bissinger's book, which profiled the

NFL Hall of Fame and Alabama's high school connections

Player	NFL Team	Hometown	Pos
Buck Buchanan	Kansas City	Birmingham	DE
John Hannah	New England	Albertville	OL
Ozzie Newsome	Cleveland	Leighton	TE
John Stallworth	Pittsburgh	Tuscaloosa	WR
Bart Starr	Green Bay	Montgomery	QB

NFL No. 1 Picks in the Draft (from Alabama High Schools)

NFL Team	Year	Pos.	Player	High School	College
Washington	1948	QB	Harry Gilmer	Woodlawn HS	U. of Alabama
Kansas City	1963	DE	Buck Buchanan	Parker HS	Grambling
Tampa Bay	1986	RB	Bo Jackson	McAdory HS	Auburn
Atlanta	1988	LB	Aundray Bruce	Carver-Montgomery HS	Auburn

NFL Retired Numbers and Alabama's high school connections

No.	Player	NFL Team	High School
86	Buck Buchanan	Kansas City Chiefs	Parker HS
73	John Hannah	New England Patriots	Albertville HS
15	Bart Starr	Green Bay Packers	Sidney Lanier HS

economically depressed town of Odessa, Texas, and its heroic high school football team.

Black has been a professional actor since his junior high days when he first played opposite Billy Bob Thornton in the critically acclaimed *Sling Blade* in 1996 at the age of 12. He has been in several movies (*All The Pretty Horses*, *Crazy In Alabama*, *Cold Mountain*, to name a few) and TV series including *X-Files* and *Chicago Hope*. He was filming *The Fast And The Furious: Tokyo Drift* in early 2006.

Michael Papajohn was a standout running back and outfielder at Vestavia Hills High School under legendary Hall of Fame coaches Buddy Anderson (football) and Sammy Dunn (baseball) in the 1980s. He then went on to play in the outfield for LSU's NCAA championship baseball team.

It was while he was a student-athlete at LSU that Papajohn got his start in a prosperous acting career. He was Dennis Quaid's stunt double in the filming of the 1988 movie *Everybody's All-American*. That launched a Hollywood stuntman career that included work in such films as *Waterboy*, *Titanic*, *Money Talks*, and *Starsky and Hutch*.

He has also landed major roles in such films as *Charlie's Angels*, *The Longest Yard* (2005), *Spider Man*, *Terminator 3* and had a major hand in bringing the filming of the movie *Rustin* to Alabama where the high school football scenes were filmed at Vestavia Hills and Thompson high schools.

NFL great Kenny Stabler, who prepped at Foley High School in Baldwin County, had parts in two popular movies, *The Indian Runner* (1991) and *The Legend of Grizzly Adams* (1990).

Former Heisman Trophy winner Vincent "Bo" Jackson of McAdory High School not only juggled major league careers in baseball and football but also found time to find work in Hollywood. His best role was that of Sgt. Clyde Packer in *The Chamber* with Gene Hackman. He also was on the TV series *The Sentinel* and *Diagnosis Murder* among others.

NFL Statistical Leaders and Alabama's high school connections

Year	Player	NFL Team	Hometown	TDs
1955	Harlon Hill	Chicago-NFL	Florence	9
1952	Harlon Hill	Chicago-NFL	Florence	12

Year	Player	NFL Team	Hometown	Pass Yds
1976	Ken Stabler	Oakland-AFC	Foley	291-194-17-2,737-27
1973	Ken Stabler	Oakland-AFC	Foley	260-163-10-1.997-14
1966	Bart Starr	Green Bay-NFC	Montgomery	251-156-3-2,258-14
1964	Bart Starr	Green Bay-NFL	Montgomery	272-163-4-2,144-15
1962	Bart Starr	Green Bay-NFL	Montgomery	285-178-9-2,438-12

Year	Player	NFL Team	Hometown	Pass Receptions
1974	Ozzie Newsome	Cleveland-NHC	Leighton	89-1,001-5
1961	Jim Phillips	Los Angeles-NFL	Alex City	74-1,092-5

Year	Player	NFL Team	Hometown	Pass Rec Yards
1974	John Stallworth	Pittsburgh-AFC	Tuscaloosa	80-1,395-11

Year	Player	NFL Team	Hometown	Interceptions made
1966	Bobby Hunt	Kansas City-AFL	Lanett	10-112-0
1961	Billy Atkins	Buffalo-AFL	Millport	10-158-0

Year	Player	NFL Team	Hometown	Sacks
2000	Trace Armstrong	Miami-AFC	Birmingham	16.5

Year	Player	NFL Team	Hometown	Punting
1961	Billy Atkins	Buffalo-AFL	Millport	85-44.5 Long-72

Year	Player	NFL Team	Hometown	Punt returns
1997	David Palmer	Minnesota-NFC	Birmingham	34-444-0 Long-57
1995	David Palmer	Minnesota-NFC	Birmingham	26-342-1 Long-74
1979	Tony Nathan	Miami-AFC	Birmingham	28-306-1 Long-86

GADSDEN'S "SEASON OF MIRACLES"

The defining moment of Gadsden's 1986 "Miracle Season" came by strange circumstances.

Coach Vince DiLorenzo's Tigers had opened the year with a win over city rival Litchfield. Injuries, first to starting quarterback David Taylor, then to tailback Gerry Benson, took their toll, however.

And after five straight losses, Gadsden was facing arch-rival Etowah in the first area game of the year.

"We needed to win a game," said DiLorenzo. "I was more worried, though, about keeping the team together and not folding the tent, so to speak. I still believed we could win. We had talked all the time about believing in yourself and believing in the team concept.

"You always wonder when working with young men are they really listening" Are they really paying attention?"

The game with Etowah was close right before the half when Gadsden was facing a fourth down at the Etowah 8-yard line. DiLorenzo, a coach who played for legendary Nick Hyder at West Rome, Ga., in high school and later in college for Charley Pell at Jacksonville State, said he decided the team needed to get some points so ordered his team to kick a field goal.

"Then the strangest thing happened," he said. "Instead of getting ready for the kick, our kids called timeout and started waving for me to come onto the field."

DiLorenzo said he found some hungry and determined faces when he got to the huddle. "Let us go for it," said split end John Massey. "Throw me the pass, and I'll score."

The young coach said he marveled at the confidence and desire of a team that was 1-5 with five straight losses. "I think they felt I was giving up on them by kicking a field goal," he said. "They were begging me to practice what I had preached. They were telling me to believe in them."

DiLorenzo agreed to let them go for it. "When I ran off the field to the sideline, all my assistant coaches had backed up some. I know they thought I had lost my mind."

A slant pass from Taylor, who had returned to the lineup by midseason, to Massey was complete. The receiver got hit at the 3, DiLorenzo said. "He should have been stopped right there, but somehow he got into the end zone.

"Right then and there is when I think this team finally came together. That's when the state championship we won later that season finally began to take shape."

Gadsden went on to win the game 16-13—with tight end Doug Baker running a post out route on a 40-yard TD pass from Taylor with less than a minute to play for the winning score.

That miracle win set into motion seven more miracle wins in a row—culminating with the 1986 Class 5A state championship.

Gadsden beat Fort Payne in week nine 7-0 to go 2-0 in the area when the defense stopped the Wildcats four downs inside the 10-yard line and recovered a fumble in the end zone as time was running out.

On week 10, Gadsden downed city rival Emma Sansom 10-6 to win the area title. Down 6-3 with a couple of minutes to play, the Tigers drove the length of the field and scored the game winner on Rodney Callaway's 7-yard run in the final seconds.

With a 4-5 record heading into the playoffs, Gadsden advanced first by beating Guntersville 18-14 on a 90-yard pass from Taylor to Dunican Caselberry with 23 seconds to play.

"That was an amazing play," said DiLorenzo. "It was just another example of these kids truly believing in themselves."

In the second round of the playoffs Gadsden drew powerful Athens—one of the state's top-ranked teams. Three times the Tigers defense stopped the Golden Eagles inside the 10 on fourth-down plays—shutting down Athens on 12 plays within the shadow of the end zone in a 10-9 win. Benson kicked the winning field goal and extra point, and returned to the team as a kicker when he was no longer able to play running back.

The third week of the grueling playoffs was a 14-9 victory over Cullman. Again the defense rose up and stopped the opponent on fourth-down tries twice late in the game.

In the semifinals, Gadsden took on powerful Pell City, quarterbacked by future NFL star David Gulledge, on Thanksgiving night, and won 9-7. A standing-room-only crowd estimated at more than 11,000 watched the upset.

There was an incredible hush after Taylor connected with Baker on the same wing-T post route they ran versus Etowah—resulting in a 30-yard touchdown with just 23 seconds left to play.

"Their defensive back jumped high and the ball went just over his fingertips into Larry's hands," said DiLorenzo. "It was like something divine was happening to these kids. All along, I enjoyed coaching this bunch of boys. They were such a super group of kids, one with no real stars. They all pulled together and good things really started happening for them."

In the finals, Gadsden beat Homewood 13-7 in the finals and finished the unlikely season 9-5. Patriots tight end Chris Gray, who went on to play at Auburn University, then had a long career in the NFL highlighted by his start on the offensive line for Seattle in Super Bowl XL some 20 years after the prep finals.

When interviewed on national television, Gray told the millions watching his biggest disappointment was losing to Gadsden in the 1986 finals.

It brought back fond memorials of that miracle season for DiLorenzo.

"What happened after that Etowah win was just incredible," said DiLorenzo. "I had been taught to believe in the impossible by my own coaches like Coach Hyder and Coach Pell. But that night when we were 1-5, my kids taught me a lesson in believing."

THE FUMBLE

CENTRAL-TUSCALOOSA VS. LEE-MONTGOMERY, 1992

Lee, ranked No. 1 in the nation at the time, was leading Central-Tuscaloosa by 14-10 with just over a minute to play and had the ball on the 1-yard line.

Generals head football coach Spence McCracken said his offensive coordinator Jimmy Perry called "747," a safe play to senior Fred Beasley that required the talented tailback to leap over the top of the line and into the end zone.

A touchdown would sew up the game no doubt. And Beasley, who went on to star at Auburn and in the NFL with the San Francisco 49ers, was perhaps the nation's top all-around athlete—a praise he would later prove when he won the AAU national decathlon championship that following summer. A high school Parade All America selection, Beasley would play in the NFL Pro Bowl in 2003.

"Jeff Bazemore handed off to Beasley," said McCracken, "and Fred leaped high. The ball squirted right out of his arms though and landed in the arms of a Central defensive back Markeelus Milligan. Coach Buzz Busby, who was their coach, later told me that Milligan was the fastest kid on their team.

"When he caught the ball, the kid just stood there for a moment kind of shocked. He was about two yards deep in the end zone. When he took off running, we had just one kid who had a shot at getting him, our quarterback Jeff. Their kid eluded Jeff and I just stood there and watched as he went 102 yards for the touchdown."

Lee did get one more chance to tie the game following the kickoff, but a 50-yard plus field goal was no good with one second left and the national championship dreams of the 1992 Generals were gone for good.

The game featured two of the state's finest prep running backs ever. Beasley finished with 86 yards on 22 carries and scored twice. Central's Dennis Riddle, who later played at Alabama, had 93 yards rushing on the night. He led the Crimson Tide in rushing in 1995 and 1996. Milligan would play collegiate ball for Stillman College.

Lee did regroup, however, and won the their second straight Class 6A state title to finish 14-1. McCracken, who was named the 1986 national coach of the year, kept the video cue set on that fumble for the next several months. When someone would visit his office, he'd tell them, "I know what you want to see, so here it is."

He'd turn on the tape and watch the horror all over again.

"[The national championship] just wasn't meant to be I guess," said McCracken. "That play [747] was one of our best. And Fred was so talented and could sky.

"I couldn't be disappointed with the season though. We won the state championship because our kids were able to put that nightmare behind them. They did a better job of that than we coaches did."